The Dreamer Cometh

by

WILLIAM A. CARLETON

WIPF & STOCK · Eugene, Oregon

Wipf and Stock Publishers
199 W 8th Ave, Suite 3
Eugene, OR 97401

The Dreamer Cometh
The Luther Rice Story
By Carleton, William A.
Copyright©1961 Baptist Convention of New England, Inc.

Softcover ISBN-13: 978-1-5326-8851-5

Hardcover ISBN-13: 978-1-5326-8852-2

eBook ISBN-13: 978-1-5326-8853-9

Publication date 4/3/2020
Previously published by Home Mission Board,
Southern Baptist Convention, 1961

LUTHER RICE
Pioneer in Mission and Education

1961 Graded Series of
Home Mission Studies

OUR BAPTIST HERITAGE IN MISSIONS
WALKER L. KNIGHT, *Editor*

Titles in the Series:

BLUE FLOWER by Jacqueline Durham
For Primaries

SAWGRASS MISSIONARY by Elizabeth Provence
For Juniors

NO GREATER HERITAGE by A. B. Cothron
For Intermediates

HIS TO COMMAND by Harold E. Dye
For Young People

THE DREAMER COMETH by William A. Carleton
For Adults

TEACHER'S GUIDE
One for each age group

iv

TABLE OF CONTENTS

Chapter		Page

v

PROLOGUE

*"Behold, this dreamer cometh. Come now therefore
. . . and we shall see what will become of his dreams."*
(Gen. 37:19-20)

THESE WORDS OF Joseph's brother are those of
the materialist who prides himself on being a practical, matter-of-fact man of the world. To such a man
the dreamer is a babbler — a visionary fanatic who cannot
see the stern realities of life which prevent the realization
of his vision.

Little that is worthwhile is done in any area of life
unless someone first dares to dream. One must take
care how he despises a dream. If that dream is born in
the purpose of God, it will surely come to pass even
though the dreamer dies and the vision seems to fade
from the memory of man. History's pages are filled with
the stories of such fulfillments.

Luther Rice was a dreamer. His vision of all the
churches of the Baptist denomination in America united
in one great endeavor to promote the whole program
which Christ committed to his churches seemed a wild,
impossible scheme in 1812. Those nurtured in Baptist
ecclesiology and traditions saw the difficulties as he, a

recent convert to the Baptist faith, could not see them. Perhaps he never recognized all of the adjustments necessary for such a plan to become effective.

Rice came to know the Baptist leaders of all parts of the United States more intimately than any man of his day. It would have greatly distressed him to know that dissension within the denomination would result in a disruption in the General Missionary Convention of the Baptist Denomination in the United States for Foreign Missions which he did so much to form in 1814. Although he was a native of Massachusetts, some of his closest ties were with brethren in the South, and he had no room in his thinking for sectionalism. Therefore, it would certainly be incorrect to say that he envisioned the formation of the Southern Baptist Convention, which came into being in 1845.

Nevertheless, his attempt to broaden the activities of the General Convention to include work other than foreign missions gave impetus to the idea of a true denominational body.

It is certain that he did not understand exactly the type of organization that must be formed to make possible the mighty, co-operative endeavor which today is embodied in the Southern Baptist Convention. Perhaps he was not the first to have such a dream, but he was the man chosen of God to spread the vision among the Baptists of America, to supply the incentive to draw them together, and to make the dream so desirable in the minds of many that at last it came true.

FOREWORD

Imagine having an intense calling to missions but no one to help you fulfill that call. That is the situation that Luther Rice felt as he and Adoniram Judson arrived in India to serve as missionaries. Having been sent as Congregationalist missionaries from New England, but having converted to a Baptist understanding of Christianity along the way, they found themselves without a sending agency.

At the time Baptist churches in the United States were scattered both geographically and organizationally. The lack of organization kept Baptists from supporting the missionary duo. As a result, Judson remained in India while Rice returned home to rally Baptists to the missionary cause. Rice spent the rest of his life helping Baptists realize they could accomplish far more by working together than they could by having each church work in isolation. Not everyone agreed with his ideas, but in the end, his ideas became pervasive in Baptist life.

That cooperative missionary zeal still burns in New England Baptists today. As a growing network with more than 350 churches across the six New England states, the Baptist Convention of New England finds great joy in owning the birthplace of Luther Rice. Our office and training center sits on the former homestead. The restored house, barn and blacksmith shop of the Rice family continues to serve as a place of training and respite for pastors, missionaries and lay leaders.

The Rice family has a rich history and remarkable heritage, but the story is not yet over. Every day Rice's dream of Baptists becoming more effective by working together is lived out by those who continue to serve Baptists around New England and around the world.

We hope you will enjoy reading about Luther Rice's life and ministry. We invite you to come and visit his birthplace and see where the dream began.

Dr. Terry W. Dorsett
Executive Director
Baptist Convention of New England

Note: 100% of the royalties from this book go to support the Rice Memorial Fund, an endowment that helps maintain the Rice Homestead in Northborough, MA. Donations can also be mailed to: Baptist Foundation of New England, ATTN: Rice Memorial Fund, 87 Lincoln St, Northborough, MA 01532

I

MEET THE DREAMER

His eyes looked out across the years,
He heard the promise, saw the plan;
A dream from God dispelled his fears,
And gave him confidence in man.

AN AIR OF TENSENESS increased steadily as the meeting continued. For three days the crowd listened to speakers and participated in the business discussions in a perfunctory manner. Their attitude plainly indicated an impatience for the arrival of some more interesting feature of the program.

The 1815 annual session of Elkhorn Association had attracted an unusually large number of visitors and messengers. Such associational meetings were still the only means by which Baptists could express themselves as a demoninational group. Only one year before, an organization had been formed in Philadelphia called the General Missionary Convention of the Baptist Denomination in the United States of America for Foreign Missions, but here in Kentucky there was a great question in the minds of many Baptist leaders about the wisdom of such a body.

The moderator was tempted to prolong his speech of introduction. For the first time since the meeting opened, there was full attendance and deep interest in the proceedings, but he could clearly see that no one was

1

listening to his words. All eyes were on the man he was presenting. Suddenly giving up the effort to bring in a few remarks of his own, he motioned to the visitor from Philadelphia and said, "Brother Rice will now address us on the subject of missions."

Luther Rice, after an arduous journey by horseback, had arrived only an hour before. He was caught by surprise at the abrupt introduction. He arose slowly and silently faced the crowd for half a minute or more. His gaze passed over the congregation, and he appeared to note each person individually. He seemed unconscious of the hundreds of eyes fastened upon him with interest and curiosity, mingled with open suspicion and distrust.

The assembly saw a tall, pale-looking young man whose earnest appearance testified to his sincerity and zeal for the cause which he represented. His pallor was the result of the strenuous journey he had just completed, but as he entered the pulpit his weariness seemed to drop from him and he stood erect with ease and dignity. He was somewhat better dressed than the average Baptist preacher, but there was nothing about him to suggest the fastidious. He made a favorable impression even before he began to speak. He did not have the "New England look" which westerners often associated with duplicity and chicanery in money matters.

Just before the moment of silence became oppressive, he quietly announced his text and subject, "Thy Kingdom Come." His manner of speech lacked the bombastic and rhythmic qualities which characterized much of the preaching of that day. His voice was low — even to those seated near him, and he neither screamed nor roared. Yet those in the very back heard him distinctly, and he held his audience to the end of a sermon lasting more than an hour.

Few men have been so blessed in their ability to sway an audience. His manner was so pleasing, his voice so appealing, and his enthusiasm so contagious that he seldom experienced any difficulty in compelling attention. William F. Broadus stated that he doubted whether Rice, as a minister of the gospel, had been equalled in the United States. He was using a favorite theme in this initial Kentucky appearance. As he spoke, he seemed to keep continually in view a glimpse of the glory of God. One who often heard him said, "This was his great peculiar characteristic—a thirsting for the advancement of the glory of God. 'Thy kingdom come, thy will be done on earth as it is in heaven' seemed to be the constant and the fervent aspiration of his heart."

Even the most violent enemies of missions were caught by the spell of his message. One such spoke later in admiration of his art and pathos but added, "I was more amused by his ingenuity than edified by his discourse."

But there were few who could escape being carried along with the gifted preacher as he pleaded for sincerity in praying the model prayer.

"How can one pray for the coming of the kingdom while he refuses to do the bidding of the king? How can we say we love our Lord and still refuse even to attempt to carry out his last command? Forgive us, Lord, that so long we and our fathers have tarried in seeking to bring the light of the gospel to the regions shrouded in darkness! Come with me, my brethren, to distant India and look at what my own eyes have beheld of the degradation and vileness which openly reigns in lands where the blessed kingdom influence has never reached."

And then, with superb skill, he took his captured audience to another land and caused them to behold the wretchedness, misery, and depravity of the multitudes. His ability to quicken the imagination with vivid word pictures brought before them the sin and suffering of people in distant lands that had never known the quickening power of Christ. Few of his hearers had ever been so far away as the Atlantic coast, and his message carried them to a totally unfamiliar world. But he was telling of that which he had witnessed, and the ring of sincerity which came from his heart convinced the most skeptical.

"How can we remain indifferent when the salvation of immortal souls hangs in the balance? There seems to be no other way in which the gospel can, according to the present constitution of divine Providence, be conveyed to the numberless millions of poor perishing heathen but by missionary labors. I do not mean by this remark to limit the Holy One of Israel. None will doubt that God can convert the heathen nations by an immediate exercise of his almighty power without using means or instruments; but is this the way in which deity has determined to spread the gospel of his glorious grace? What has been the manner of operation heretofore?

"When a faithful and zealous missionary was needed to preach among the Gentiles the unsearchable riches of

Christ, by an astonishing display of sovereign grace he converted the zealously persecuting Saul and sent him upon this important business; and if in those days there was need of missionaries to go forth among the heathen preaching to them the gospel of peace which bringeth salvation, it is not less necessary and important for missionaries to be sent among them now."

"This also seems to be fully evident from the Holy Scriptures. The great apostle and, as I may so say, missionary of the Gentiles, reasons thus: 'How then shall they call on him in whom they have not believed, and how shall they believe in him of whom they have not heard, and how shall they hear without a preacher, and how shall they preach except they be sent?' Let those who dare to speak against the missionary interest beware lest they be found to fight even against the eternal Jehovah."

John Taylor, a Kentucky pastor, respected and loved for his consecrated, sacrificial spirit, had wrought faithfully and conscientiously for the Baptist cause. He half rose from his seat among the ministers at the front. No one had worked more fervently to win Kentucky for Christ, but through prejudice and lack of education he had taken a violently anti-missionary position. Ordinarily, he would have been given an immediate hearing, but a glance at the crowd made him aware of the folly of attempting any type of diversion.

The pleading note in the speaker's voice changed to one of triumph, still mingled with overtones of pathos. He told how the people of God throughout America were responding to the mission appeal, how scores of

Baptist congregations were opening their purses to support the work in distant lands.

"The very angels are rejoicing at the liberality of God's saints, and it is now our privilege to join with our brethren in thus glorifying our Redeemer. Who is on the Lord's side?"

He ceased to speak, but all present felt that the service was not yet ended. One of the deacons sitting in the back arose, and with deliberate motion, placed a fifty-cent piece in his hat and silently passed it to his neighbor. In a few moments, a number of hats were being circulated, and when the collection was finished some $200.00 had been contributed to the cause of foreign missions.

For the first time, the missionary question was a burning, vital issue among the Baptists of Kentucky. Rice's recent tour of the seaboard states had aroused the churches east of the mountains to a decision concerning the Christian's part in spreading the message of redemption. Now his visit to the Baptists of the West was acting as both a unifying and decisive factor among the churches and associations.

No one could hear him and remain unmoved. Some were aroused to fierce and bitter opposition, while others listened as if he were an angel from heaven. Few preachers have ever aroused such enthusiasm, and few have provoked such intense resentment.

The response of the great associational assembly at this, his first visit to Kentucky, is typical of his reception everywhere in the West. No longer could Baptist churches be indifferent to the mission call. He presented the need, urged the duty enjoined upon them by the Scriptures, and advanced a plan that called for a decision to demonstrate a willingness to obey the divine command. All this was done with such telling effect and power that almost immediately the lines were drawn between the missionary and anti-missionary forces.

At the close of the meeting, people met in groups and discussed the message and the messenger. A large number were convinced the speaker had spoken the truth and the new General Missionary Convention was indeed a plan God's people could use to carry out the plain teachings of his word.

But others saw in this proposal for sending out missionaries something anti-scriptural and even sacrilegious. One of the more influential and able preachers who held to this latter position soon had a crowd about him as he sought to refute the challenging message to which they had listened.

"All of that story of the suffering and ignorance in foreign lands is very touching, but what does that have to do with religion? The moral government may have an obligation. Educating the heathen and improving their lot might be a good thing for our civil government to sponsor, but let us not dishonor the cause of religion with such things. The principle and practice of the nation's system is according to the spirit of the world and not according to the spirit of the gospel. The mission advocates say their principle is good because it is to send the gospel to the heathen and by that means have heirs of glory begotten. Just so, I might say my neighbor, a friend, is very wealthy and wants an heir very badly and I, viewing his wealth and how happy his heir would be, join with his anxiety to divide his happiness with his heir. Would it not be a good principle to wish he had an heir? Yes, but a most horrid act for me to attempt to become the father. Just so, we all agree the object is good, and we can truly say, 'Oh, that the heathen were all saints,' but for us to step in the place of God to send means to accomplish the birth of these heirs must be horrible and wicked. They are like old Sarah who could not wait for the birth of the promised heir according to the Lord's promise but must give her handmaid to her husband."

Not many in Elkhorn Association could accept such hard hyper-Calvinistic argument. Rice's powerful appeal to the scriptural teaching concerning the use of means to accomplish God's purpose was too fresh on their minds. They were in the habit of preaching the plan of salvation to the lost and urging upon them the duty of seeking the Lord. To accept the idea that God does not use human means in the great work of redemption would be to repudiate their former doctrine and practice. But the matter of sending out foreign missionaries through the agency of a national organization of Baptists was something entirely new.

Many were eager to hear the opinion of John Taylor whose influence counted for much among his brethren. An enthusiastic young man stated that Rice was evidently a man chosen of God to usher in a bright and new day in Christian history.

Taylor cleared his throat to show intense disapproval and said, "I fear it will be a new day indeed but hardly a bright day. I see two dark clouds hanging over our Baptist Zion. One betokens subjection to godless mammon, and the other foretells the loss of sovereignty of Baptist churches as they are merged together in one big super-ecclesiastical machine. They make it sound mighty pious, and some of them may even believe it is the work of God. The truth is, it is a mercenary plan of priest-craft. Money and power is the watchword of the whole scheme, aiming at lordship over God's heritage."

"But Brother Luther gives us scripture for his teaching," the young man began.

Taylor interrupted, "Brother Luther, as you call him, succeeded in his purpose. He received a great sum of money for his fine speech, and he tied one more strand about our churches. That name makes me think of some history I read about a servant of the Pope of Rome who came to Germany to fleece honest people of their money under the guise of religion. A man named Luther rebuked him and stood fast for the liberty of a Christian man and sent old Tetzel scampering back to his priestly backers. We have the names mixed up today. Rice should be called Tetzel, for he is practicing the same cunning art as the Pope's old orator. They tell me he won't speak at an association unless they let him take up a collection.

"With his sophistry and Yankee art, he is out to get money for missions — but don't be deceived, he gets a part of all he receives. He is making merchandise of the people through feigned words and from the strongest symptom of covetousness. A false teacher loves money. Tetzel's operations were when the Pope of Rome and the Mother of Harlots were at their zenith. Rice's movement bespeaks the man of sin or men of sin in embryo, and Baptist associations — too soon — may become adopted daughters of the old Mother of Harlots. Money and power were the signs of the times when the mystery of iniquity began to work in the days of Paul. The same principle is plainly seen in the great Board of Missions in America, in Rice, their chief cook, and also in their mighty convention. It is time to sound the alarm to all the American Baptists."

These severe charges were made with an earnestness matching that of Rice himself. None who heard Taylor doubted his integrity. In his earlier ministry he had tasted the sting of persecution set in motion by centralized ecclesiastical bodies and had come West to preach amidst the privations and hardships of the frontier settlements rather than endure the galling restrictions imposed upon Baptists in some of the Atlantic states. Many of his hearers had seen Baptist preachers imprisoned in Virginia. Connecticut still had a state church establishment, and only recently had such an establishment been abolished in Massachusetts. Moreover, history seemed to teach that as local congregations merged their interests in an all-inclusive larger body, they inevitably lost their own autonomy.

It is not remarkable that Taylor's words were so effective. Even those who accepted Rice's message most wholeheartedly had certain reservations and doubts. He did not have for his purpose merely the organization of local missionary societies or even of one great society for foreign missions. Such a procedure would not have encountered too much serious opposition; but he addressed churches and associations as if it was their Christian duty to place first in their program of activities the evangelization of the world. He seemed to conceive of a New Testament church as a missionary society devoted to the carrying out of the Great Commission in co-operation with all other New Testament churches.

Even more alarming was his tendency to consider so many activities as phases of this great missionary program. He constantly referred to education, evangelism, and publication work as mission enterprises and seemed to have no doubt that all of them should be promoted by the newly organized convention. So certain was he of the correctness of this view that he seemed unable to grasp the tremendous difficulties in the way of such a scheme. His vision called for the entire denomination working together to promote the whole program of Christian advance. In vain, it was pointed out to him that the Baptist teaching of the independence of the local church would prevent their entering into an arrangement in which their endeavors would be channelled and directed by their representatives in a denominational convention. He believed the two principles — church autonomy and united endeavor — were not contradictory and the people of God could work together in a plan that would keep inviolate both precious principles.

To a Southern Baptist living in 1961 it seems strange

that Rice should have faced such stern opposition. His idea was merely that all New Testament churches should work together in seeking to obey the Great Commission in its entirety. Yet, in his day, the idea was a novel one. Many people had manifested great zeal in promoting some particular work, but never within the memory of that generation had Baptists been so arrestingly challenged to a unified effort in carrying on all phases of the kingdom work.

The associations existed for the purpose of fellowship. The organizations or societies formed for service sponsored only one activity and were based not on churches but on the individual. No wonder earnest souls who heard Rice speak asked, "How can such things be?"

But the missionary himself had no doubts about the future of the cause he championed. He was as confident of the outcome as if he had a clear confirmation of the defeat of the anti-mission forces. At the close of the evening session he, with three other visitors, went home with a local pastor to spend the night. They sat up late drinking coffee as Rice told one interesting story after another. He seemed perfectly relaxed and wholly unconscious of the scalding criticism being heaped upon him in other similar gatherings. Many of his tales were filled with keen humor and brought on gales of laughter. Some of his friends thought his wholesome story-telling indicated a spirit of levity not quite in good taste for a minister.

He loved fellowship with friends; he had a keen sense of humor; and he was not one to worry, because he had an absolute trust in the complete triumph of righteousness.

Throughout his life as a Christian he observed seven daily prayer periods. He spent as much time thanking God for his mercies as in asking for blessings. The vision of a united, zealous missionary spirit was in his heart, and he was certain of its fulfillment. Before the vision could be transformed into reality, some common missionary agency must be formed with access to the churches. There must be created a working force willing to do what needed to be done in any neglected area which falls within the bounds of the Redeemer's charge to his people. The aim of it all must be the founding and developing of New Testament churches in the entire program of Christ both at home and abroad.

There were other Baptist dreamers. In Boston, Thomas Baldwin dreamed of a foreign mission society supported by Baptists of all the nation. In Philadelphia, William Staughton dreamed of a great Baptist institution of learning, the equal of Yale or Princeton. Isaac McCoy dreamed of Indians by the thousands coming to Christ, and John Mason Peck had his heart warmed with the vision of a Baptist empire in the West. Rice's dream combined them all into one. His was the glorious vision of a united denomination taking the whole of God's message to the entire world.

Many who loved him best shook their heads sadly over the disappointment which they felt confident was coming to him. He was to them a dreamer — a visionary. His beautiful dream was impossible. They were correct in their forecast of the immediate future, although the General Missionary Convention, called by many the

Triennial Convention, had partially brought it into reality. He suffered defeat and failures that would have broken the faith of most men, but he kept his dream when others thought it forever destroyed. It was not his privilege to witness its later fruition. He died in 1836 before the reality of his dreams. In 1845 when the Southern Baptist Convention was organized, the first glimpse of the beginning of the realization of his dreams began to be visible.

II

THE DREAMER AT WORK

No mystic dreamer far remote
From needs so old yet ever new;
He dreamed, but let the wise man note
He worked to make his dream come true.

A MAN OF LESSER FAITH would have remained at the associational meeting and publicly replied to the criticisms of his missionary appeal. Some of the most ardent friends of the cause sought to persuade Rice of the wisdom of such a procedure, but he was needed in other places. By sunrise the next morning he was in the saddle, bound for another annual associational meeting.

As the horse followed the trail through the verdant hills, the mind of the rider planned for the future. Convinced of the truth of his message, he had no doubt God was working to arouse the Baptists of the United States to a sense of corporate denominational consciousness and a realization of their missionary responsibility. The difficulties of such a goal made little impression, for his entire life had been beset with difficulties. The years ahead were to bring ordeals and trials, but his faith was never shaken. Perhaps as he rode he permitted himself a brief glance toward the past and cheered his heart with memories of the never failing presence of the Comforter. In his homeland, in foreign countries, and on the high seas he had tasted the joys of fellowship with the Lord, and he was persuaded that every moment of the thirty-two years he had lived upon this earth had been ordered of God.

Leaving him to journey to his next appointment, let us take a rapid survey of his life and refresh our minds with the evidence of God's leadership.

Captain Amos Rice, of Northboro, Massachusetts, happened to be at home on March 25, 1783 when Sarah, his wife, bore a son. The captain was often absent, and since his violent temper and inconsiderate habits did not serve to contribute to the harmony of the family circle, such absences were not necessarily unwelcome. Nothing indicates he was greatly impressed with the advent of Luther, his ninth child. Nor did subsequent happenings in the life of his son ever cause the captain to feel he was greatly honored in being the father of such a Christian leader.

The Rice family was descended from William the Conqueror, and the members were inclined to value prowess on the battlefield far more than skill in religious work. More than fifty of them served in the Revolutionary War. Captain Amos made a good record in the conflict, participating in some of the most famous battles. He also participated wholeheartedly in the more sordid camp activities, but his courage and patriotism were never questioned. Like most of the family Captain Rice considered it a pleasure to prove both courage and patriotism in combat upon the slightest provocation. With all their excess of pugnacity the Rices were a prolific, hearty, and long-lived family. Amos and Sarah had only ten children, but many of them had far larger families. Luther's death at fifty-three was undoubtedly premature, brought on by the intense way he drove his body in his arduous labors.

Both Captain Rice and his wife were affiliated with the local Congregational church, but neither took any interest in church activities. Luther was nineteen years old before he was converted and united with the congregation. In his boyhood he displayed the family traits of independence and courage, although he did not inherit the love for physical combat. When only sixteen years old, he became interested in a business venture having to do with timber for ship building. Hearing that lumber was plentiful and inexpensive in Georgia, he made a trip to that state, without taking the trouble to inform his parents, and was away for more than six months!

Soon after this escapade, young Luther began to reflect seriously upon his spiritual state. He had memorized passages from the Scripture and had studied the Westminster Catechism since childhood. He understood well enough the theory of God's salvation, but he became concerned that he had never experienced its reality. The Northboro pastor advised him to unite with the church and lose his worries in the external forms of religious life. Such advice Luther could not accept, and his deep sense of conviction continued to burden him until his health was impaired and his friends feared for his sanity. The climax came in 1802 after a struggle lasting almost two years.

His own account of this deep depression and of its joyous ending is as thrilling as Augustine's account of his surrender to Christ. After relating his awful sense of sin and condemnation, he tells of his joyous assurance of salvation:

"At length the period of deliverance drew nigh . . . And then I found in this disposition of absolute unreserved submission to the will of God, a sweet and blessed tranquility.

"From that moment I seemed to be on the Lord's side —was no longer at variance and in quarrel with my Master; and from that day to this, I have entertained a hope that through the abundant mercy of the Lord, and the rich grace of the precious Redeemer, and the power of the Holy Spirit, on the ground of the great atonement, I have been reconciled to God! And I may say, too, to a very happy extent, this hope has remained invariable and unshaken. My feelings often vary, and vary much; but not my hope . . . This happy experience took place one Saturday evening, in the fall of the year, a little after sunset; I do not recollect the day of the month; though I very distinctly remember the hour of the day, the spot where I was, and the circumstances around me."

With his traits of character he could not be content merely to be a nominal Christian. After joining the Northboro Congregational Church he sought to promote among the members a vital concern for Bible study, Christian witnessing, and soul-winning. His activities were an embarrassment to his pastor and church, for neither shared his concern. His father became angry and abusive when he sought to introduce family worship and went so far as to ridicule and accuse him of foolish and stupid acts to his fellow townsmen.

The cheerful Christian attitude so characteristic of Luther Rice's conduct in later life, void of resentment and vindictiveness, showed itself at this early stage in his Christian life. He maintained a sweet spirit toward all who opposed him. He always spoke of his father with the utmost respect and consideration. Writing many years later he indicated his belief that God used his father's opposition to release him from a bond which might have hindered his following God's plan for his life. The letter, written in 1835, has these words:

> My father . . . as well as my mother (still exceedingly dear to my memory), was a member of the same church which I first joined. While I was merely sober, serious and moral, but unacquainted with the power of vital godliness, he was well enough pleased. But when it pleased God to make me see, and feel and manifest the reality and life of religion; having never experienced . . . anything of the kind himself, he could not bear with it in me. This . . . uprooted the fond anticipation I had indulged of possessing the home place, and taking care of my parents (a consideration exceedingly dear to me) in their latest decline. And thus what might otherwise have constituted a material barrier in the way of my devoting my life to the sacred service of the ministry, was actively removed. How mysterious are the ways of Divine Providence.

When he sought to hold prayer meetings in the homes

of his acquaintances, he found them unwilling to receive him. In later years he delighted to recall that of the two homes which remained open to him for such services one was that of a Baptist who lived in a neighborhood not far away. This seems to have been his first association with a member of the denomination for which he was to perform such monumental service.

A neighboring minister, who was sympathetic with Rice's fervent evangelistic spirit, became interested in the young man. Observing his faithfulness and cheerfulness in trial he encouraged him to believe that God was leading him to some place of particular usefulness in the Redeemer's work. Rice acknowledged a feeling of God's call and entered Leicester Academy to begin his educational preparation for the ministry. After three years of preparatory study he entered Williams College in 1807.

Even before his college days Luther was concerned with the condition of the heathen. In letters and in conversation he often expressed an anxious regard for their salvation. Soon after entering Williams he became closely associated with a number of young men who shared his views, and led by Samuel J. Mills, they organized a "Society of Inquiry on the Subject of Missions."

He had come to feel a personal obligation to go himself as a missionary. One day during a period of prayer, alone in the woods near the college, he became very burdened for God's leadership in finding his proper place of service. He had considered foreign mission work before but had about decided to abandon the idea. As he prayed that day the words of Christ, "Go ye into all the world and preach the gospel to every creature," came into his mind with such clearness and power that he resolved to spend his life in mission service, whatever it might cost.

He wrote his brother, "I have deliberately made up my mind to preach the gospel to the heathen. I do not know, but it may be in Asia."

Each member of the Society had reached a similar decision. They met secretly for prayer and discussion on the subject of missions without at first having any plans for beginning the enterprise, other than bearing witness by conversation and letters to their conviction of the missionary imperative. They were greatly interested in the American Indians and in the West Indies as well as in the Orient.

At Andover Seminary a kindred feeling was working in the hearts of a few students and having learned of the Williams College group they formed a "branch Society." Adoniram Judson was one of the leaders of the seminary organization.

Rice gave wholehearted attention to his studies. He had entered Williams with sophomore standing, and in the middle of his third year he was admitted to Andover Seminary upon recommendation of his college president. This enabled him to finish his theological training in 1811 along with those who had graduated from college a year before him. He and Judson became the closest of friends.

In 1810 the zealous young volunteers felt the time had arrived for action. When the Massachusetts General Association of Congregational ministers met at Bradford, they were presented with a memorial urging the Christian obligation to take the gospel to the heathen and requesting appointment to the proposed task. Six names were signed to the document. Before presenting the paper to the association the last two names were omitted in order that the preachers might not be alarmed at the prospect of having so many applicants. Since Rice was one of the last to sign, his was one of the names left off.

The Association was convinced that God was leading the young students, and the American Board of Commissioners for Foreign Missions was constituted as a result of their appeal. Although this Board was greatly aided by gifts from Christians of other denominations, it has predominately served as the foreign mission agency of the Congregationalists. Its first appointees were Adoniram Judson, Jr., Samuel John Mills, Samuel Newell, and Samuel Nott, Jr.

Perhaps one reason Rice consented for his name to be stricken from the petition was the difficulty of a personal problem. He was engaged to a Christian young woman who was unwilling to leave America for the foreign field. Rice's love was genuine and he felt bound by the betrothal agreement, but he was convinced God willed that he should be a missionary. He sought to win her to a willingness to share with him in following his sense of divine leadership. For months he hoped for a favorable answer, but at last she told him in definite terms she would never leave America and, if he felt he must do so, he could consider the engagement broken.

His sorrow was assuaged by the realization that now

he could carry out his plan to preach the gospel in India, if he could only persuade the Board to appoint him. It was January 28, 1812 that he requested the presidential committee of the Board to certify his appointment.

His request was impossible, the committee explained, since they had not been given the authority to appoint missionaries. Since the ordination service was scheduled for February 6 there was no time for a meeting of the full Board. Then, too, there were no funds to care for his passage and maintainance.

For five days he pleaded his assurance of God's call and his conviction that God would make it possible for him to go, if the committee would give their consent. At last they could resist him no longer. The committee voted to assume responsibility for his appointment if he could raise the money for his passage and complete equipment.

Traveling on horseback in the rigor of a New England winter Rice cheerfully visited churches and friends to solicit contributions. His assurance was justified, for in six days he arrived at the Tabernacle Church in Salem, Massachusetts, for ordination with the necessary funds.

The service, the first of its kind in America, attracted considerable attention. Rice, almost completely exhausted by the exertions of the past days, was much impressed with the solemn ceremony and always recalled it with a thrill of spiritual fervor. The time seemed very unfavorable for such a journey. Besides the winter weather, feeling was strong against England. An embargo was being imposed and war seemed eminent.

On February 15 it was decided Rice would not sail from

Salem with the Judsons as planned, but would leave from Philadelphia three days later on the *Harmony*. The sailing was delayed until February 24, and it was June 8 before the ship arrived at the Isle of France. After some 20 days, they sailed to Calcutta, and there on August 10 Rice rejoined Judson and his party. The voyage had been a trying one, and Rice was very sick upon his arrival in India. His physical illness was equalled by his mental disturbance upon learning the Judsons had adopted a Baptist position. On the first Sunday of September they were baptized in the Baptist chapel in Calcutta. This brought back to Rice's mind doubts and uncertainties which he had vainly tried to forget.

In his college days he had studied the subject of baptism with a Baptist friend and had concluded that mode and subject were non-essential and that he would continue his Congregational affiliation. Two English Baptist missionaries, companions on his voyage to India, had talked often with him about baptism, but he reached Calcutta with his mind unchanged.

However, the Judson's decision moved him greatly. On September 17 he heard Judson preach and made the following record in his journal:

> Attended chapel service in the forenoon; Brother Judson's text was Matthew 28:29, Go ye therefore and teach all nations, etc. His object was to show what is baptism, and to whom it is to be administered. I have some feeling and difficulty on this subject, which I find myself reluctant to disclose to my brethren; may the Lord himself lead me to his own right way.

Rice was too frank to conceal for long his desire to arrive at a certainty concerning the matter. He began eagerly to talk with both Pedo-baptist and Baptist friends and to spend much time in prayer for divine guidance. He determined not to allow his affection for the Judsons to influence him. He writes:

I have just mentioned that Brother Judson has become a Baptist. As I have here with him considerable means for this purpose, I am endeavoring to investigate thoroughly the subject of the sacred ordinance of baptism. What may be the result of this inquiry, I am not able at present to say; but from the progress already made I conceive it to be possible that a revolution in my own mind, similar to that which my dear brother and sister have experienced, may take place. Should this be the case, I shall in all probability, go with them to Java. It would be peculiarly pleasing to me to be associated with them in the mission, but my affection for them can by no means determine me to become a Baptist without conviction that Baptists are in the right; nor can I on the other hand, be deterred from my conscientiously examining the subject, nor from following what really appears to be the truth; notwithstanding my unpleasant considerations attending such a change of sentiment in my situation. And it is a principle with me, that truth can be no loser by the most rigorous examination, provided that examination be conducted in the fear of God with a desire to know the truth, and a disposition to do his will. May the Lord himself lead me in the way in which he would have me go.

As the weeks passed he became convinced he must

make the same decision the Judsons had made. He came to believe baptism should be administered only by immersion and only to those who have professed a personal faith in Christ. On November 11, 1812 he made this entry in his diary:

"Was this day baptized in the name of the Holy Trinity. The Lord grant that I may ever find his name to be a strong tower, to which I may continually resort and find safety."

In a letter written the next day giving an account of his baptism he wrote, "It was a comfortable day to my soul."

However, many things about the immediate situation did not contribute to the feeling of comfort. He and Judson joined in writing at once to Dr. Worcester, secretary of the American Board which had sponsored them, telling of their change of doctrinal convictions. This change in sentiment on the subject of baptism was naturally unwelcome news to the Congregational board. There was not a great deal of Christian spirit manifest in doctrinal controversy in those days, and little consideration or kindness was shown these missionaries who had deserted the board which had appointed them. Even such a publication as the *Quarterly Theological Review* questioned the sincerity and integrity of Judson.

At first the Americans considered the possibility of offering themselves for appointment by the English mission society. They discussed this with the British Baptist missionaries at Serampore, but all concluded such a course would be unwise, even if they could be assured their offer would be accepted. Dr. William Carey was very emphatic in his belief that the situation afforded an opportunity to arouse the Baptists of America to assume a responsibility to foreign missions, and a direct appeal should be made to them. A letter was sent to Dr. Thomas Baldwin, pastor of the Second Baptist Church of Boston, Massachusetts, and editor of the *Massachusetts Baptist Magazine,* apprising him of the unusual situation and expressing the hope of support from the Baptist churches in America.

About this time the British East India Company informed the American missionaries they must leave India, and orders were given for their deportation. The door of Burma seemed closed, and the three found passage back to the Isle of France where they waited and prayed for God's guidance. The outlook was extremely dark as they sought for an open door. They were more than a thousand miles from their fellow Baptist missionaries from England and three times as far from their own country.

Having submitted their resignations to the American Board of Commissioners for Foreign Missions and disassociated themselves from the English Baptists, they faced an uncertain future, not only in the field where they were to serve but also in financial support. They had little acquaintance with the Baptists of the United States and no assurance as to what response might come from them, but they had an assurance in their hearts that repelled all fears.

Rice wrote, ". . . we were three solitary individuals

disconnected from all the Christian world; in a heathen land with but scanty means of a very temporary sustenance; but we did not doubt that the Lord would provide for us!"

As they prayed for direction and carefully considered every aspect of their situation, the three decided Rice should return to America and enlist American Baptists in the mission cause, while the Judsons sought for a suitable field in which to work. Immediately an opportunity occurred for Rice to secure passage back to America, and this was accepted as God's endorsement.

During the two months' stay on the Isle of France Rice's health had improved and he seemed well able to undertake the long voyage home. The *Donna Maria* on which he sailed was bound for South America, and he accepted this as an opportunity to investigate the possibility of mission work on that continent. The vessel arrived in the harbor of St. Salvador on May 4, 1813, and not until July 17 was he able to obtain a passage to the United States. He spent the intervening time in the home of the American consul, whose wife he offended by his refusal to christen her children.

On September 7, 1813, the ship entered New York harbor. The young minister stood quietly on the deck, oblivious to the bustling activity of the sailors as they prepared for the mooring. As he stared at the buildings along the shore his thoughts went to scores of other cities and towns and the people whose interests and affection he must enlist. Not one word had he heard from either Congregationalists or Baptists since he had written concerning his change of sentiments.

It is doubtful if anyone in the crowd on the pier was impressed with anything unusual in the young man who stepped eagerly down the gang plank. The burning urge within him would result in the shaping and drawing together of a great denomination. The dream in his heart was of no interest to those about him, and the look of anticipation in his eyes could easily have been attributed to an expected reunion with some dear one from whom he had been long separated. No one met him, and so far as he knew no one in all the country shared his vision. Yet his return to America was destined to have results which still are being felt after 150 years. Dr. W. H. Whitsitt said, "The coming of Luther Rice was the most important event in Baptist history in the Nineteenth Century." The truth of this statement is even more evident today than when spoken more than seventy years ago.

Rice planned to leave at once for Boston to attend the meeting of the American Board on September 15. He felt it would be proper to appear before that body and in a respectful manner relate his and the Judsons' experience, and thus terminate the relationship in an orderly way. But he decided to take time to at least introduce himself to the Baptists of New York City.

He walked slowly along the street leading from the waterfront, pondering on the best means for making some contact with his fellow Baptists. A pleasant looking man in front of a small shop greeted him with a cheery "Good morning." Impulsively he stopped and, after a comment on the beauty of the day, asked, "Do you happen to know any Baptist people here in the city?"

"I certainly do," was the quick reply. "Two Baptist ministers have been customers of mine for more than ten years. Are you a friend to Parkinson or Williams?"

"No. I know few Baptists, although I am happy to be a member of the group."

"Baptist or not, you have surely heard of William Parkinson. He served three terms as chaplain to the United States Congress and preached each Sunday in the Capital. The members of Congress crowded to hear him and President Jefferson missed only one service during those sessions. The First Baptist Church is fortunate to have such a pastor. I am not a Baptist, but I hear him often. However, the Oliver Street pastor is the Baptist preacher I enjoy most. He is a fiery Welchman who thinks Christianity ought to be spread all over the world. His name is John Williams, and he is always interested in travelers from foreign parts."

These words were like an answer to prayer to Rice. Having secured the address he made his way to the Williams' home, where he arrived just as the minister was preparing to leave the house.

"My name is Luther Rice and I—" he began as he saw the courtly gentleman standing in the doorway with his hat in his hand.

"Luther Rice! I have been wondering when I should have the pleasure of meeting you. You have come at a good time. Our missionary society is meeting this evening, and you can speak to us and tell us what we can do to help in the work to which God has called you. Come in. I shall postpone my trip downtown until this afternoon."

He showed Rice into the study adjoining the living room and began plying him with questions concerning the Judsons, the attitude of the East India Company toward Christian missions, and kindred subjects.

"Wait, my brother, until I adjust my thinking," Rice pleaded. "I did not know that American Baptists had missionary societies, and I was not certain that my name was known to any of them."

"Your name is known to many of them. Dr. Thomas Baldwin is not one to keep a secret — at least one that contains such good news as that conveyed in the letter he had from you and Judson. We were so thrilled to learn of it here in New York that we almost had our missionary society in operation before Baldwin got one started in Boston. The brethren at Providence were not far behind us, and inquiries on the subject of missions are coming from all over the country. Enough money has already been raised to support you and the Judsons for three years."

Rice made no attempt to conceal his elation, "You mean there are now three Baptist foreign mission societies in the United States?"

"There are at least five," laughed the pastor. "Lucius Bolles of Salem, Massachusetts, had more faith than the rest of us. He organized the Salem society before we had any news of missionaries who would be willing to be sponsored by the Baptists of America. Since then another has been started at Haverhill."

The remainder of the morning they talked concerning the possibility of opening Baptist mission work in South

America as well as India and Burma. In the afternoon steps were taken to inform the Baptists of the city of Rice's presence. Two evenings later he met with the local mission society and was greatly encouraged by the keen interest in world-wide evangelism.

"The Baptists of this land must be far more missionary-minded than I realized," he said to Williams as they walked to the preacher's home after the meeting.

"You must not think that what you heard tonight is typical of our people. Only those who are ardent believers in the cause of missions are members of the society. You would not have such an enthusiastic response if you should accept my invitation to preach to our church next Lord's Day. Many of our best members are completely indifferent and some are violently opposed to the idea of foreign missions. There are few churches that would back such a program. The best plan is not to attempt to make missions a feature of church life. The friends of missions are free to organize themselves as they see fit apart from the church fellowship."

The pastor seemed to see nothing unusual or wrong in the idea, and Rice soon learned it was accepted by most Baptist leaders. There was something about it that did not seem quite right to the champion of missions, however. It was not that he objected to the idea of mission societies. Both in England and in America, and among other denominations as well as Baptists, it was the customary way of supporting the work.

The disturbing phase was the idea that missions were something apart from the work of the church. Since the command to take the gospel to the entire world is so clearly taught in the Scriptures he felt it ought to be promoted clearly and continuously in the churches. He was soon to find most people did not agree with him. One of the most prominent leaders, an advocate of missions, insisted any obligation to promote any cause, aside from the local church, was an individual cause and had nothing to do with the church itself. He was fond of saying, "People show their love for Christ in different ways. One may be just as good a Baptist in refusing to join the missionary support as in associating himself with it."

Four days later Rice arrived in Boston, and on September 15 appeared before the American Board of Commissioners for Foreign Missions. He sought to explain his change of belief on the subject of baptism and requested his connection with the Board be terminated. He was given no answer, either then or later, but he was informed the next day by one of the members that his relationship to the Board had ended, since Rice himself had terminated their agreement when he was immersed. The treasurer had been instructed to request that Rice return the money expended on his outfit and passage to India, even though he himself had raised these funds.

He spent the next few days visiting the Baptists of Massachusetts, and urging them to a united effort in a great mission program. The last week in September, the Boston Society held a meeting with Rice as an honored guest. Visitors were present from the Societies at Salem and Haverhill. Rice was given eager attention as he pleaded for a concerted missionary drive on the part of American Baptists.

"We are well able to do a more mighty work than has ever been attempted in our day. British Baptists with some 500 churches averaging 100 members, have impressed the world with their faithful endeavors. Here we have twice as many Baptists. If we were united in the Redeemer's work we could shake the kingdom of evil. Surely you, who have already shown such love and devotion to the mission can lead in organizing Baptists of this land to obey Christ's command!"

Dr. Daniel Sharp, secretary of the local society, was very optimistic about the possibility of arousing a deep missionary concern. He questioned the wisdom and expediency of any delay in perfecting an organization. One of the visitors agreed with him. "All that is needed," the visitor affirmed, "is that our brethren be stirred up to a remembrance of their obligations, and that some channel be provided for transmitting their benevolences to those appointed to serve in foreign fields. The Boston Society could well act in the latter capacity. Let Brother Rice travel throughout the states with his heart-warming message. Societies can be set up wherever he goes, and the money they raise can be sent through this Board to sustain the missionaries. The interest and experience of these missionary-minded leaders and their location here at a port from which ships go out to all parts of the world make an ideal arrangement. Both time and money could be conserved by this plan."

Rice could see the logic of such reasoning. Such a proposal, if accepted, would make it easy for those already interested in missions to make their interest felt. But his dream of a united denomination could not be realized by such procedure. He was relieved as others raised questions about the matter.

It was finally decided the wisest plan would be for Rice to make a circuit of the states, bringing the mission appeal and seeking counsel of the brethren in various sections concerning the best procedure in implementing a mission program.

The next few months were among the happiest in all Rice's life. Wherever he went he was welcomed with enthusiasm. Great crowds listened to his moving description of heathenism as he had witnessed it. He became the most talked-of Baptist in America, and through his exertions more than twenty Baptist missionary societies were founded before the year ended.

He was delighted with his visit to the annual meeting of the Philadelphia Association. There he met William Staughton, pastor of the Sansom Street Baptist Church of Philadelphia, who had been present at the historic meeting in Kettering, England, when the first Baptist foreign mission society was formed.

This great association, the oldest in America, was unhesitating in its endorsement of Rice's appeal. Some of the leaders expressed a deep interest in some type of general organization to draw Baptists together in their common task. The fear and distrust of such a body, which was so evident in New England, was not present here. Philadelphia Association had long before discovered churches could work together in a larger organization without sacrificing their sovereignty.

Rice next turned southward where he met with the same reception he had received in Philadelphia. As he talked with Baptists throughout the country he became convinced that God was leading in a far greater plan than the mere organizing of local missionary societies. He came to believe an over-all denominational alignment could be devised that would be representative of the churches through associational and state bodies.

In Charleston, South Carolina, he met Richard Furman, pastor of the First Baptist Church. Dr. Furman was a wealthy man of learning and was recognized as the leading Baptist of his state. His formal sedateness seemed at first to indicate a cold dignity not usually associated with Baptist ministers. This mistaken impression was soon dispelled when one heard him preach and came to know the warmth of his great heart.

He encouraged Rice in his hope for a denominational organization. "We ought to combine for the sake of work in other areas than missions. I have long felt that Baptists should have a theological seminary, but no one church or association could found such a school. Perhaps this appeal of yours may be the very thing we need to bring us together. When you visit Savannah Association, be sure to talk to my young friend, W. B. Johnson, about this idea of yours."

The Savannah Association was in session when Rice arrived. They had heard of his coming, and he was welcomed to the meeting, which he addressed with his usual success. The Savannah Society for Foreign Missions was formed immediately, but something of far greater importance took place in connection with his visit.

As he discussed with the gifted Johnson the hope for some better way to enlist Baptists of America in a worldwide mission, he struck the heartiest response he had encountered.

"Why postpone the initial step?" his host asked. "Let a call be sent for a meeting in which a workable plan can be devised that will be acceptable to our people. Dr. Furman and I have often talked of uniting the Baptists in a single state, but your scheme has much more liklihood of success. The Baptists of Philadelphia are respected by our brethren everywhere. Persuade them to invite interested delegates from Baptist bodies to meet with them next spring."

Rice wrote immediately to Staughton, and within a few weeks the announcement of a meeting to consider giving "vitality to that union of exertion" was received by Baptist associations, churches, and mission societies from New York to Georgia.

On Wednesday, May 17, 1814, the meeting was held. Thirty-three people were present, of whom twenty-six were ministers. They came from eleven states and the District of Columbia. By Saturday afternoon a constitution had been adopted and the General Missionary Convention of the Baptist Denomination in the United States of America for Foreign Missions had become a reality. Richard Furman, who had a prominent part in writing the constitution, was elected president.

The Baptists of America now had a "convention"

although its field of labor was restricted to foreign missions. It recognized itself as a denominational body. The constitution provided that "religious bodies of the Baptist denomination" who contributed at least $100.00 per annum could be represented in the sessions, which were to be held triennially.

Since that memorable meeting Baptists' interest in missions has continued to grow. True, there had been rumblings of opposition in some quarters, but Rice was certain of continued success as he rode through Kentucky on his journey back to Philadelphia.

His mind was busy with plans for enlarging the scope of the convention work. In his months of labor among the churches he had come to believe that foreign missions could not be successfully advanced without a corresponding advance on the home field in education and evangelism. His dream was growing as he worked to make it come true.

III

THE DREAMER DISCREDITED

The vision seems to fade away;
To hold it firm he vainly tries;
How strange, that at the close of day,
It still seems real before his eyes.

THE JOURNEY TO Philadelphia for the first triennial meeting enabled Rice to visit a number of associations and mission societies. His popularity continued to increase in spite of intense opposition which showed itself even among those who claimed to be friends of missions, but who were antagonistic to his ideas about promoting missions.

The long ride to Philadelphia gave Luther much time for serious reflections on the subject so dear to him. His mind was busy with plans for enlarging the work of the convention and for increasing its supporting constituency.

His first annual report was about ready to be presented to the Board. It was so encouraging and so filled with news of mission activity that he determined to have it printed. He could distribute it as he visited churches and other Baptist groups. "I shall have to buy a sulky in which to travel so I can carry such literature," he mused. As he shifted his travel-weary body in the saddle he smiled and said aloud, "Such an improvement in the way of a conveyance will not be entirely unwelcome."

His travels would have broken the health of a less robust man, and it was certainly wise to secure some easier mode of transportation. An illustration of the extent and constancy of his journeying is given in a four months' report quoted in James B. Taylor's *Memoir of Rev. Luther Rice.*

Attended the Philadelphia Association (October 1818) and hastened to the Dover Association, meeting in King and Queen County, Virginia. Preached, took collection amounting to 272 dollars; made a circuit through Maryland and Pennsylvania to the Saulisbury Association, Delaware, consuming two weeks. The next Saturday and Sunday were spent in Fredericksburg, Virginia and the following Sunday in Raleigh, North Carolina. Crossed the country to Lynchburg, Va., thence to Romney (now W. Va.) and reached Pittsburgh; thence to Washington, Pa.; Wheeling, Zanesville, Chillicothe, West Union, Ohio; Maysville, Washington, Lexington, Georgetown, Harrisburg, Bardstown, Louisville, Shelbyville, Frankfort, Versailles, Richmond, Campbellsville, Glasgow, Kentucky; Nashville, Franklin, Murphreesboro, Lebanon, Liberty, Sparta, Knoxville, Jonesboro, and Blountville, Tennessee; Fincastle, Lynchburg, Lexington, Staunton, Harrisburg, New Market, Luray, Milford, Front Royal, Zion, Winchester, Charlestown, Harper's Ferry; thence to Fredericktown and to Lancaster, Pa., and back to Philadelphia on February 2.

His extreme good nature was never overcome by fatigue or sickness. He took every criticism without rancor and usually with a smile. On one point only did he seem peculiarly sensitive. Once a sour-faced critic said with a sneer, "If you were so interested in the heathen, why aren't you in Burma with your friend, Judson, instead of enjoying the comforts of life here?"

Even this unjust and unkind cut brought no retort. Only the flush which reddened his face showed the stab of pain it brought to his heart. It had been more than two years since he said goodbye to the Judsons, expecting soon to rejoin them. After the organization of the General Convention, the Board appointed him a missionary but instructed him to remain in America and continue his efforts to arouse the Baptists of the United States to a greater interest in missions. It was not intended that he stay here long. He wrote the Judsons, "I hope to get the Baptists so well-rallied in the course of five or six months, that the necessity of my remaining will no long exist."

With the passing of months he came to have a larger conception of the steps necessary to enable a denomination to become a vital missionary force. His idea of distributing the printed report was improved by the establishment of two periodicals, *The Latter Day Luminary* and *The Columbian Star*. This caused some of his opponents to grumble: he was trying to make a publication society out of the Triennial Convention. Rice had, by this time, come to think of the printed page as indispensable to the mission program. In his mind publication work was simply a phase of missions.

There were at least two other areas of service he was eager to discuss with the Board. He was remembering the contention of Dr. Richard Furman, the president of the Convention, that Baptist progress waited on education. This gifted pastor of the First Baptist Church of Charleston, South Carolina, had long sought to devise some plan for establishing a great Baptist university and theological seminary. In 1791 in a letter he stated, "But a great part of our ministers, as well as members, are very illiterate men; which is a great hindrance to the Baptists having the weight in the state they would be entitled to, and has in many instances in the interior parts of the country, opened the door to enthusiasm and confusion among them."

When Luther Rice came to Charleston with his moving appeal for foreign missions, Furman realized such a man and message could draw the Baptists of America together in some type of corporate union. If such an organization were once formed, he felt it could be led to sponsor a much needed educational institution. He gave Rice his active support and, as has been noted, was elected president of the General Missionary Convention of the Baptist Denomination in the United States of America for Foreign Missions. From the very beginning he sought to bring education into the work of the Convention, but he realized Rice's support of the cause would be necessary if he succeeded.

Rice came to his championship of education as a result of his concern for his first love — foreign missions. He observed in his travels that the anti-mission spirit thrives on ignorance. He knew missionaries must be trained before they could be sent out, and he began to think of a great national institution in some central place for both classical and theological training. At the same time he was learning that trained ministers are necessary to the proper support of the missionary enterprise, whether they remain as pastors in the homeland or go out to work among the heathen. In his thinking, Christian education was a part of the work of missions; and it seemed perfectly proper for a missionary convention to found and maintain universities and theological seminaries.

The second area of service which he championed was also an outgrowth of his missionary spirit. In his travels he often met caravans journeying westward to find homesteads in the new territory acquired by the Louisiana Purchase. In his dream he pictured the future of that western wilderness when it would be covered with farms, villages, and cities. He saw the need for a mighty campaign of evangelism and Christian nurture among the settlers. Strong churches here at home could make possible a mightier work in the foreign field.

He progressed in his thinking until he conceived publication, education, home missions, and foreign missions as all so closely connected that one was naturally a part of the others. Why should the General Convention not do all of these things?

But many Baptists of his day did not agree with him. In an earlier day some of the associations had sent out missionaries to work in destitute areas, both among the whites and the Indians. This was an expression of a cooperative mission spirit among the churches channeled through the only denominational body then in existence among the Baptists. For a time the Philadelphia Association included churches in three states and seemingly was on its way to becoming a national denominational body, but the trend had changed. Local church independence was now so emphasized that such co-operative action among the churches, as such, was rare. The idea of a mission society composed of contributing members entirely apart from the church organization was the accepted way of supporting missions.

Rice seemed never quite able to keep this society idea clearly in his mind. In his report to the Board of his first year of service he wrote, "Two objects were particularly in view — to engage the associations in the missionary cause, and to open a chanel of intercourse between the Board and all of the Baptist churches in the United States."

By the end of his first year of service as the agent of the Convention, Rice's dream reached full maturity. He dreamed of a national denominational body in and through which the Baptist churches could work co-operatively in the areas of publication, education, home missions, and foreign missions.

The Board was divided in its attitude toward their agent's ideas as reflected in his first annual report.

Dr. Henry Holcombe, pastor of the First Baptist Church, Philadelphia, had joined with Dr. W. J. Rogers of the same city, in a letter to Richard Furman questioning both Rice's sincerity and ability. They were both vice-presidents of the Board of Foreign Missions of the Convention. Dr. Furman could not be swayed by groundless accusations, but he promised to give the matter a full hearing at the triennial meeting.

William Staughton, pastor of the Sanson Street Baptist Church of Philadelphia and corresponding secretary of the Board, concurred with Rice in the plan to establish a theological seminary. Unfortunately Dr. Holcombe in opposing Rice and his plan, also was opposing his fellow pastor, William Staughton. The Board, as a whole, decided they had no authority under the constitution either to begin an educational work or enter the home mission field. Rice was encouraged, however, by their assurance that a recommendation would be brought by the Board to the triennial meeting in Philadelphia in 1817 that the scope of convention work be broadened.

He continued his travels, and in all parts of the country was used of God to quicken the hearts of his people. In June 1815 he was the featured speaker at the session of Warwick Association meeting that year with the church at Lattinstown, New York. He preached with even more than his usual power to a very responsive congregation. Throughout his message he noted a young man seated directly in front of him, whose eyes never wandered for a moment. He leaned slightly forward as if fearful he might miss a single word. Rice's own heart was warmed by the rapt interest of his listener, and he pleaded with intense earnestness for men to surrender their lives to God's will even if it meant going to distant mission fields.

The attentive young man was the first one to clasp Rice's hand when the service ended. "I am John Mason Peck, pastor of the Baptist church at Amenia. Like you, I was once a Congregationalist, and I have been a Baptist only a little more than three years. Your sermon has

45

disturbed me sorely. Please come home with me and help me decide how I can know God's will for my life."

There was a compelling earnestness about the request that made refusal impossible. Luther Rice, the most prominent Baptist preacher in America, whose presence was clamored for in a hundred places, changed his schedule and went to be the guest of the young pastor at Amenia.

In the hours they spent together Peck bared his heart to his visitor: "When I answered God's call to be a preacher, I somehow had the feeling it was his plan that I serve him in some very special way. The text for my first sermon was Mark 16:15, 'And he said unto them, go ye into all the world and preach the gospel to every creature.' The whole theme of my message was Christian missions, and I have never been able to quench the feeling that I should be a missionary. But I have no theological training. I have improved every opportunity to secure a literary education, and in spite of my family responsibilities have prepared myself to teach school. In fact, that is my chief means of support since my church pays a very meager salary. It appears to me that a missionary ought to have that training in theology and Biblical studies that has been denied me. I know of no school where I may obtain such training, and I do not have the means to attend such an institution if there were one."

"By the time you are ready for theological study the Baptists of America will have a seminary for you to attend," Rice spoke with such assurance that the listener was led to believe plans for a Baptist thological institution

46

had already been formed, as indeed they had in the heart of this practical dreamer. "The matter of financial support can also be arranged. I am not concerned about the problems connected with your education. If you are convinced God wants you to be a missionary and you are willing to fully and completely surrender yourself to joyfully do his will, these matters will work out. Where do you feel God wants you to go?"

Peck looked somewhat ill-at-ease when he answered, "I know the word 'missionary' ordinarily means one who goes across the sea to some distant land with the Christian message. Perhaps that is what God wants me to do, but ever since my first attempt to preach I have had my eye upon the people west of the Mississippi, where the gospel is almost unknown. Of course, there are many pagan Indians there, too."

His voice trailed off into an embarrassed silence; and he was almost afraid to look at Rice, whose interpretation of missions might be very different from his own.

"Good! I have been praying that God would raise up workers to take his message to the western settlements. The West is as dear to his heart as the lands to the East, and an American without Christ is as lost as any Burmese who does not know him. Take the next four months and visit the associations and enlist them in support of the mission cause. Preach your sermon on Mark 16:15 and tell them of the General Convention and of God's call to the Baptists of America. Keep in touch with me and let us see where God will lead us."

By the last of November, Peck was able to report

47

gratifying success in his labors among the associations and a definite conviction that God was calling him to the West. Rice wrote to him on November 30, and gave him definite assurance that plans were being made to open a western mission under the auspices of the Convention at the next meeting. He advised Peck that Dr. Staughton, pastor at Sansom Street Church in Philadelphia, was conducting a theological seminary in his home, and he was certain it would soon be taken over by the Convention. Rice strongly urged the young missionary volunteer to come to Philadelphia and join the three students already studying under Staughton. Through the generosity of friends it was possible for Peck to take this step. In the ensuing months he lived with his fellow students in Staughton's home and studied under his direction all the subjects of a theological course, including Latin, Greek, and Hebrew, and in addition "listened to instructive lectures on botany and other branches of natural science."

Rice kept in close contact with his protege by both letters and visits. He was pleased with Peck's attainments and was certain the Board would not lose the chance to appoint such a man to the western field when the Convention made it possible. As the time approached for the first triennial meeting of the General Missionary Convention of the Baptist Denomination in the United States of America for Foreign Missions, there were many of Rice's friends who were not as confident of the outcome of his enlarged plans as was the optimistic originator.

On January 24, 1817, Richard Furman, president of the General Convention and pastor at Charleston, wrote to Edmund Botsford that it was probable he would not attend the meeting. He said,

> I think it will be an important meeting in its consequences, as well as its nature: either for forwarding the mission and giving rise to other undertakings highly interesting to our churches, and the cause of God; or else laying the foundation for discord and discouragement among the Baptist churches respecting schemes of concert and public utility. I fear that at Philadelphia there is a source of evil which is likely to spread its baneful influence far. In fact, I fear that Satan has taken some of our brethren there in a snare, in a manner that they are not sensible of, and that their views and feelings respecting some particular things, excite them to say and do what is directly contrary to the best interest of religion and their own, true renown; and Dr. Holcombe has now published a pamphlet against the Philadelphia Association and churches are likely to form into parties.

Fortunately he did attend the session, and his strong support helped carry the day for the friends of progress. He appointed a committee to look into the charges brought against Rice and the Board. Rev. Jesse Mercer of Georgia was chairman of the committee. The report expressed complete confidence in the action of the Board and its agent and strong disapproval of the critics.

There was a great reluctance on the part of several of the delegates to include education within the scope of the Convention's work. They maintained that the Convention had been formed to engage only in foreign

49

mission work and the sponsorship of education would harm the mission cause.

The proposed constitutional amendment was worded in such a manner as to meet some of their objections. It stated:

> When competent and distinct funds have been raised for that purpose; from these without resorting at all to mission funds, the Board shall proceed to institute a classical and theological seminary for the purpose of aiding pious young men, who in the judgment of the churches, and of the Board, possess gifts and graces suitable to the gospel ministry.

After much discussion the president called Dr. Baldwin to the chair and made an earnest plea for solemn consideration on the part of the Convention, of "the very serious and religious importance of a well-trained ministry." The delegates were impressed and the amendment was passed. To Luther Rice, this was a definite command to go forward with the establishment of a school. Dr. Furman realized this vote of the Convention was only a small flame of awakened interest which must be kindled and fed until great numbers of Baptists would be convinced of the necessity of a united effort in theological training. He was in agreement with Matthias B. Tallmadge, who wrote on May 30, 1817,

> . . . the entering wedge for the promotion of education has been so far driven that it may be hoped that another convention will be able to give effective organization and efficacy to your excellent views on this subject.

It was Furman's opinion that the Convention should

center on the idea of the theological seminary, and that smaller bodies should assume the obligation of "the education of pious young men in classical learning at places the most convenient to them: that they may be thus fitted for divinity studies and be finally sent to the theological institution."

He felt that at least $100,000.00 should be on hand for the establishment of a seminary before it was actually begun. To elect officers, contract for buildings, or employ teachers prematurely, he felt, would be harmful to the cause of Christian education. He was less assured of the willingness of Baptists to support a central educational institution at this stage of development than was Rice. He saw the difficulties of the task and felt the necessity of waiting until Baptists in general could come to share his concern for an educated ministry.

But Rice was, as usual, convinced his cause was certain of success. He was one who never took counsel of his fears, and he immediately began to labor to make the school a reality.

The matter of home missions was also discussed in detail. John Mason Peck and James E. Welch were prepared to leave for the West, and they waited with deep concern for the vote to be taken. The following amendment to the constitution was passed:

The Board shall have the power, at their discretion, to appropriate a portion of their funds to domestic missionary purposes, in such parts of the country where the seed of the Word may be advantageously cast, and which mission societies, on a small scale, do not effectively reach.

51

On May 25, 1817, Peck and Welch, in a solemn Sunday service, were set apart as missionaries to the far West, and money was appropriated for their support.

Rice's dream was being rapidly fulfilled. For the next three years he gave an increased emphasis to education and solicited funds to help young men study in Philadelphia with Dr. Staughton and Ira Chase. Chase came to Philadelphia and joined with Staughton in 1818 in what has been called "the earliest school for theological training for American Baptist ministers." By 1820 the school had an enrollment of eighteen.

The personal animosities existing among some of the Baptist leaders in Philadelphia made the city a poor location for a center of Baptist work. Then, too, there was an appeal in the idea of having a school located in the national capital. Rice enlisted the aid and support of a number of Baptists in Washington and arranged to purchase forty-six and one-half acres for a campus site, costing $6,000.00.

When the Convention met in 1820 he reported $10,-000.00 had been subscribed toward paying for the land, erecting a building, and endowing a professorship. He stated, "A building has already been commenced, 116 by 47 feet, which will contain rooms enough to accommodate 80 to 100 students. It only wants the countenance of the Convention, with the blessings of heaven, to insure complete success."

He proposed that the school offer college as well as seminary training. There was no Baptist school of college rank south of Rhode Island, and this suggestion seemed wise to the majority.

Furman was present at the 1820 session, and he must have felt as did some of the more conservative delegates that Rice was moving too rapidly. He was not re-elected as president. Instead Robert B. Semple of Virginia, a man fourteen years younger than Furman, was elected president. The enlarged program of the Convention was recognized in the change of its name to "The General Convention of the Baptist Denomination in the United States of America for Foreign Missions and Other Important Objects Relating to the Redeemer's Kingdom." Rice was asked to continue as agent of the Convention to collect funds for both "missions and education." William Staughton was named president of the newly established school now called Columbian College. The offices of the Board were moved from Philadelphia, where so much local contention had existed, to Washington; and Staughton continued to serve as secretary.

Rice and his friends were jubilant. True, there was one action of the session which was displeasing. The Convention voted to discontinue its western mission with the exception of the work among the Indians, but Luther the Optimist refused to be disturbed. He firmly believed that with educated leaders and some proper representation of the Baptist constituency, the general body would correct any mistake it had made. The western states were inclined to be more progressive than those along the Atlantic. If the influence of western Baptists could be felt in the Convention, greater progress would be made.

When the Convention met in Washington in 1823 Rice's popularity was still high. The college had officially opened in 1822, and the delegates were delighted with what they saw. Rice was officially commended for his faithful service, and the delegates acknowledged "a debt of thankfulness to their indefatigable agent, the Rev. Mr. Rice, whose attention to missionary and collegiate concerns has been steady and uniform."

So successful had he been in realizing his vision that there seemed to be only one more step to make it a reality. The Convention was now authorized to engage in missions and "other objects relating to the Redeemer's kingdom." The thing now necessary was to effect a plan that would in some way make it the agency of the churches of the denomination rather than a society composed of delegates from contributing religious bodies. Plans to bring about this transformation had been maturing for some time, and now they began to be openly advocated.

From the beginning in 1814, some had thought of the General Convention as being a denominational body through which the churches might carry out the tasks which they could not do separately. Others thought of it as merely a foreign mission society and were never in accord with the idea of making it responsible to the denomination or including other activities as part of its work. Rice, ably assisted by men such as Furman, Staughton, Johnson, and others, had steadily won in his efforts to make the body conform to their idea of a Baptist denominational organization. The lines were now being drawn for an outright contest between the opposing ideas. The question to be settled was, "Can the Lord's work be best promoted through separate voluntary societies based solely on financial contributions or through one great denominational organization based ultimately upon the churches as their influence is expressed through some definite channel of communication and representation?"

That the system then in use did not adequately provide for ascertaining the will of its limited constituency was easily pointed out. The Washington meeting of 1823 consisted of fifty-three delegates, and thirteen of them were from the District of Columbia. Rice and others who agreed with him insisted the Convention should be so constituted that it would be representative of all the Baptist churches. He had conceived of a plan for bringing this about.

In 1821 the Baptists of South Carolina formed "The State Convention of the Baptist Denomination of South Carolina." Its annual meeting was to be composed "of the several Baptist Associations in the state, who may approve the measures here adopted; and of representatives from other religious bodies of the Baptist connection concerned in the promotion of the same objects with the Convention, the number of delegates and representatives being always a just proportion to the number of their constituents." The constitution stated that the body was "to promote home and foreign missions, Sunday school work, religious education and the increase of vital, practical religion." It was also stated that the state body "should seek to co-operate with the General Convention of the Baptist Denomination in the United States and generally in aid of their important, laudable undertakings."

Here was a state body truly representative of the Baptists of the state and willing to work with the General Convention. To Rice it seemed to be the solution to the problem of securing a full constituency for the national body. Before the end of 1825 at least ten Baptist state conventions had been formed. Rice's proposal was not that society representation in the Convention be immediately stopped, but delegates should be recognized from the state conventions, which in most cases were composed of representatives from the district associations. Of course, the associations were in turn composed of messengers from the churches. He thought that ultimately, as the denominational idea prospered, the composition of the General Convention would be restricted entirely to these delegates from the state conventions.

Other voices were raised in support of this or some similar idea. Francis Wayland had written in the *American Baptist Magazine* a stirring plea for a "general union of our Baptist churches throughout the United States." He contended, "a missionary society is not a representative body, nor can any one of them speak the language of a whole denomination."

The plan he advocated was that the churches transmit their funds and desires through the associations to the state convention who would send delegates to meet in a national convention.

In April 1826 just before the triennial meeting another lengthy article appeared in the same magazine advocating the same plan. The writer, who signed himself "Candidus," pointed out that at the last meeting in 1817 there were five more delegates from the District of Columbia than from all New England. He affirmed that a convention based upon the state conventions would be truly representative of American Baptists. He closed his argument with these assertions concerning such a convention:

Those who attended would each *in fact* represent the feelings of that portion of our churches by whom they were delegated. The General Convention would thus become a strong bond of connection between all the different portions of our own denomination scattered over this widely extended country, and would bind them together in, it may be hoped, indissoluble union. The General Convention being thus composed of delegates from the State Conventions, and the State Conventions being composed of delegates from the Associations, and these last of delegates from the churches, it would be the heart to the whole system and might send the pulse of healthy influence to every church and to every individual in the land.

This sentiment in favor of reshaping the General Convention into a denominational body based on state conventions seemed to prevail everywhere. Since most of the state conventions sponsored all phases of the denominational program, such a step would have been the culmination of Rice's labors. This action was so taken for granted when the state convention in Massachusetts was formed in 1824, provision was made in its constitution that when a national convention should be formed for state conventions the newly constituted state body should "send delegates to meet in such a convention."

The fifth triennial meeting of the General Convention met in the building of the Oliver Street Baptist Church in New York City. It was in session for twelve days, and its actions were a complete reversal of what might have been expected in the light of the apparent sentiment referred to above. Not only was there no broadening of representation, nor any closer connection with the churches, but Columbian College was separated from the Convention, which was henceforth to confine its work solely to foreign and American Indian missions! The man who was most active in leading the Convention to take such action was Francis Wayland, who only a short time before had written so eloquently on the other side of the question!

It is very difficult to secure all of the facts necessary to a full understanding of what caused this surprise overthrow of the plans Rice had so long promoted. Richard Furman had died the year before, but it is doubtful if his presence could have prevented the Convention action.

An examination of the list of delegates present in 1826 reveals the lack of true representation of the Baptist denomination in the meeting. This weakness in the organization had been clearly pointed out. "Candidus" had said in his article in the *American Baptist Magazine* that the representation "arrangement is most manifestly unjust. Your readers will imagine as well as I can describe the evils with which an active and intriguing man might bring upon the Convention by an abuse of this arrangement. I hope the time will never arrive when any man among us will be disposed to intrigue in the cause of Christ."

Of the seventy-two delegates in attendance, forty-four were from New England and New York. Only eight were present from the District of Columbia, and only eleven from all the southern states. It was among the Baptists of New England and New York that opposition to Rice and his plans had suddenly crystalized, and with such an attendance of delegates there could be no doubt concerning the issue.

The two groups who united to sway the Convention were the foes of Columbian College and the champions of the "society method" of promoting mission work. In some cases the same individual was a member of both groups. In any case they were willing to work together in the common purpose of reshaping the Convention into a foreign mission society.

When Columbian College was first proposed there were few Baptist schools in existence, and the idea of a national Baptist educational institution seemed highly desirable. But now the states were coming to feel the need for colleges nearer to the local scene. Hamilton Theological Seminary opened in Hamilton, New York, in 1820, and out of it came Madison University and Colgate Academy. The state convention of New York was solidly behind the Hamilton school and quite naturally did not desire money to go from their state to support a college in Washington. The Baptists of Rhode Island had a similar attitude toward Brown University of which Francis Wayland became president in 1827.

The financial affairs of Columbian College were in a very deplorable state, and the situation was seized on by both groups who opposed Rice. The trustees, led by the ever-hopeful agent, had contracted debts in a building program and on operating expenses. A severe financial depression had seriously curtailed the collection of funds. The college had won the approbation of many national political leaders, and its president served as chaplain of the House of Representatives. When Lafayette came to America in 1825, Columbian College acted as host at a reception given for him in Washington. But all of this could not care for the debt which was steadily mounting.

In desperation the trustees went so far as to request Congress for a loan. The senate rejected the request by a vote of twenty to eighteen. It is strange that Baptists should have so contradicted their own beliefs concerning the separation of church and state as to have made such a request.

Rice was making every effort to secure contributions and evidently forced his body beyond all endurance. He became seriously ill and for several days seemed very near death. It is little wonder that the story was soon current that he had diverted mission money for the use of the college — a story the falsity of which has long since been clearly established.

Many great leaders of the foreign mission movement were citizens of New England, with more of them living in Massachusetts than any other state. Boston was a center of interest in the work, and many people were persuaded the board in charge of mission operations should be located in that city and directed by men, who through long experience and demonstrated devotion to the cause, were eminently qualified for the task.

It was, therefore, the aim of those in control of the 1826 Convention to divorce the Convention from all work except foreign missions, to continue the system of society representation then in force, and to remove the offices of the Board to Boston. They had all the votes necessary to take these steps, and yet a week went by before definite action was taken involving these matters.

The leaders knew that winning the vote would not be sufficient. Rice was too popular with the rank and file of Baptists, and they realized that if he still maintained his popularity he could arouse the denomination. Therefore, they began maneuvers to cast doubt on both the integrity and efficiency of the man who had done more than all the rest to awaken American Baptists to a sense of the world-wide mission. A number of committees were appointed to report on the financial affairs of the college, the matter of mission collections, the condition of the *Latter Day Luminary* of which Rice was editor, and other matters on which some charge of misconduct on the part of the agent might be based. As a final gesture, a committee "on the conduct of Mr. Rice" was appointed!

These reports were made by men opposed to Rice's dream of a great denominational organization, and it is natural the reports were slanted to question his fitness for the offices he held. In spite of all their efforts, not a single legitimate accusation could be brought against Rice, but by baseless insinuations and the twisting of words their purpose was accomplished. A resolution of censure was voted! When the Convention adjourned he had no official position connected in any way with either Columbian College or the foreign mission movement.

It is easy for men in our day to sit in judgment on Baptists of more than 100 years ago. In the light of our knowledge it is easy to see that they were wrong. An honest study of the reasons motivating them appears to prove the sincerity of their motives even if we doubt the justification of the methods they used.

They were alarmed over the drop in mission contributions for the past five years and blamed it on the incorporation of other activities into the program of the Convention rather than on the over-all financial condition of the nation. They argued that people who are interested in some particular Christian endeavor such as foreign missions, home missions, Christian education, etc. should band themselves together to promote that one object. There would thus be no division of interest and the leaders would become specialists in their field. People will give more generously, they contended, to some definite cause in which they are concerned than if that object be joined with some other for which they have little or no regard.

This feeling was strong in the North Atlantic states. With it was the fear that a convention based on state conventions and providing proportionate representation would take from places of leadership those best qualified to serve. The eastern distrust of the crude frontier spirit west of the mountains, which was beginning to show in the nation's political life, had its counterpart in religious circles.

The New York and New England delegates were overwhelmingly successful in their political maneuvers. All of the officers elected were from New England except the president, William Staughton, then of Washington but formerly of Philadelphia. The offices of the Board were moved to Boston. Dr. Lucius Bolles was elected corresponding secretary, Francis Wayland recording secretary, and Heman Lincoln, a prominent Boston layman, treasurer.

Rice's dream seemed dead.

IV

THE DREAM LIVES ON!

So he continued still to show
The dream of service sent from him;
He made the hearts of others glow;
They followed though the light grew dim.

THE CHORES WERE finished, and the ordinary daytime activity connected with plantation life in Virginia in 1826 had slowed to a lazy stop. Inside the comfortable dining room of the farm called Nordington, Dr. Robert B. Semple, the preacher-farmer, leisurely ate his evening meal while bringing a report to Ann, his wife, on his recent trip to New York City. Dr. Semple often found it necessary to travel great distances in the interest of his denomination. He had served as president of the General Convention of the Baptist Denomination in the United States, and it was to attend its triennial meeting that he had made the trip to New York.

"I now have one of the most difficult tasks I have ever attempted," he said. "Not only am I president of the board of trustees of Columbian College, but I have also agreed to serve as financial agent of the school. The amount owed by the college is large, and it is going to be difficult to secure enough funds to keep the institution going. Mr. Rice had a greater load on his shoulders than any of us realized."

"I gather you are not sympathetic with the way Rice was treated in New York," Ann remarked. "It must have crushed even his cheerful spirit to be so mistreated as you report."

"It is of great concern to me that I did not have the chance to visit with him after the meeting. I really fear for his health as well as his spiritual condition."

There was a disturbance in the direction of the stable and soon footsteps were heard coming up the path. A voice called from the porch, "Am I in time for supper at the Semple table?"

The couple at the table gazed at each other in unbelief. There could be no mistaking that voice, and yet it was difficult to accept the idea that the subject of their conversation was entering their home when they pictured him as hundreds of miles away.

Dr. Semple arose quickly, and passing the Negro servant who was grinning broadly, met his guest in the middle of the entrance hall. "Luther Rice, you are as welcome as you are unexpected," he said warmly. "I heard no carriage. How did you come?"

"Columbus pulled the sulky and me at the usual pace. I think we made the best time we have ever made from New York to Virginia. I actually believe that horse gets faster as the years fly by. I drove directly to the stable without coming up the main drive to the house. In that way I unharnessed Columbus and had him fed before the boys came racing down to see who had arrived. I kept them from announcing my presence so I could have the fun of surprising you."

Mrs. Semple had darted into the kitchen at the first sound of Rice's voice, and now food and another pot of coffee were speedily in evidence. She called the men to come to the table, and soon the interrupted meal was resumed.

Rice seemed in good spirits. It was not apparent in his manner that he had undergone such a cruel experience only a short time before. He talked of Columbian College with all the animation of former days, and casually referred to an offering for foreign missions which he had received two days before and had already forwarded to the Board in Boston.

He noted the puzzled look on Semple's face. "Yes," he said, "I am still working at the same task — collecting money for missions and the college and trying to promote the welfare of the whole cause of Christ. The fact that neither the Convention nor the trustees is paying my salary is not going to change my life's work."

A look of pain appeared on his face for just a moment, but it was speedily followed by a merry laugh. "The truth of the matter is that I am in a better condition salary-wise, than I was before. Half a dozen of my friends have promised to supply my needs, so I am six times better off! Besides, I shall not have to work any more with those tedious reports. I shall merely send in the money I collect and call that report enough."

Semple saw his friend was announcing his plans for the future. A few questions brought out the facts already indicated. Several of those who were sympathetic had encouraged Rice to continue as an unofficial agent of the college and the Convention. Some very close to him resolved to see that he had the necessities of life, so all he collected could go to the cause so dear to him.

"I am placing the college first in my appeals just now, for by helping it we can best help the entire field of mission work. That is why I am here. I have a contribution to turn over to you. Here is a bank draft to the amount of $3,500.00 to help wipe out that deficit."

"Whom did you talk into making such a gift?" Semple queried.

"A friend of the college," said Rice, trying to avoid looking his host in the face.

A look of understanding came over Semple's countenance. Someone had said something to him recently concerning a legacy that had come to Rice from his parents' estate. As the conversation continued he drew out the whole story. Rice's lifetime savings of some $500.00 had been added to the inheritance.

"It is not right that you should give all that you have to a cause that others, equally obligated, refuse to support. I admire your generosity and your Christian spirit, but I doubt the wisdom of your judgment," Semple said sternly.

"Brother Semple, God has blessed you with a wife, for whose sake you would unhesitatingly give all you have in material goods, and even your life. I am wedded to Columbian College for life. I shall gladly live for it, or die for it, as God wills."

There was a definiteness in Rice's words that seemed to make any refutation useless. His voice was as solemn as

Semple's, and no one hearing him could doubt his determination and his earnestness.

When he left the next morning he was his usual merry self. He lingered at the breakfast table for the fourth cup of coffee and told a humorous story of an embarrassing experience while visiting in a Connecticut Baptist home. On that occasion when he called for his fourth cup of coffee, the servant girl said, "You've drunk your cup, the missus' and the master's, and there's no more."

Unlike weaker men who crumble under defeat and rebuffs, Luther Rice continued to show the steadfastness and Christian spirit which he had always exhibited. There was no lessening of his radiant faith in the wisdom, goodness, and power of God. He refused to allow hatred or a desire for vengeance to poison his heart, and continued to work with cheerfulness and assurance.

For the next ten years he was constantly on the road. He refused to become a victim of self-pity. When someone spoke of his lack of a home he replied that he had dozens of homes. An excerpt from a letter he wrote to Judson elaborates on this theme in the following:

> These homes, as I frequently call them, are exceedingly dear to me. None but a pilgrim, literally 'sine domo' as one of my brethren addressed me in a letter, can realize how sweetly precious they are. One of these where I frequently find rest and comfort, as did the prophet in the kindness of the good woman who had a chamber built for him upon the top of her house, is the home of Brother William H. Turpin, of Augusta, Georgia, which place is . . . my southern headquarters for the winter.

The letter then refers to the residence of Jesse Mercer of Washington, Georgia; Archibald Thomas of Richmond, Virginia, and Dr. Cullen Battle of Powelton, Georgia, as being other homes which were his. In these homes he found love for himself and sympathy for his plan of general denominational work. It was in the southern states that he was given the warmest welcome, now that he had been discredited by the Convention. The Baptists of the South had been from the beginning more inclined toward the idea of a corporate denominational body than had those of the North. Rice's continued activity among them could not fail to make more vivid this conception.

The closing years of Rice's life were filled to the last with the labor and privations of an itinerant agent. He faced bad roads, inclement weather, and the hardships of travel through sparsely settled country. Each night he faithfully recorded in his journal the events of the day, and then spent hours writing letters to people in the interest of missions and the college. His body began to show the strain of this continual exertion, and in 1832 he suffered a slight stroke. He was warned a more severe seizure might come at any time. He replied, "I am ready—but I should like to bring up the college first."

As his physical strength began to wane he lost some of his bouyant light-heartedness. In 1835 he wrote to a friend that he was endeavoring to correct "the habit of lightness, pleasantries, foolish talking, and jesting, in which I have so long and so shamelessly indulged."

He continued to push himself, traveling, writing, and preaching. In 1836 he was journeying through South

Carolina on a fund raising tour for the college. On August 28, at Elam, he preached his last sermon using the text from Acts 8:35, "Then Philip opened his mouth and began at the same scripture and preached unto him Jesus."

When he reached Edgefield he was too ill to go farther, and he was taken to the home of an acquaintance, Dr. R. G. Mays. He grew worse in spite of the ministrations of his friends.

After a period of unconsciousness he asked the doctor if his condition was critical. On being told he was indeed dangerously ill, he said, "Send my sulky and horse and baggage to Brother Brooks, with directions to send them to Brother Sherwood and say that they all belong to the college."

On Saturday, September 25, 1836, he died quietly in his sleep. He was buried near the Pine Pleasant Baptist Church not far from Edgefield, South Carolina.

News of his death was received with sincere sorrow in those areas where he was known and loved. A great crowd packed the auditorium of the First Baptist Church of Richmond, Virginia, to hear J. B. Jeter bring a memorial tribute. Another service was held at Columbian College in Washington.

The Religious Herald and the *Biblical Recorder* published accounts of his death with appropriate expressions of appreciation for his sacrificial and useful life. Other periodicals joined in his praise, but the official organ of the General Missionary Convention of the Baptist Denomination was reluctant to follow their lead. At last, in the December issue of 1836, there appeared the following notice:

The Rev. Luther Rice, one of the earliest missionaries of the board, and for several years the indefatigable agent of the General Convention, died in Edgefield District, South Carolina, September 25, after a short illness, in the fifty-fourth year of his age.

Rufus W. Weaver, in *The Place of Luther Rice in American Baptist Life,* points out that Rice seemed in one sense to be a complete failure. He failed to win the hand of the girl he loved. He was never permitted to return to the foreign field as he so desired. The Convention which he was responsible for forming repudiated his plans for a denominational body and reverted to earlier conception of a foreign mission society. Even Columbian College soon passed from Baptist hands, and few recall that he had anything to do with the institution now known as George Washington University.

But time has justified the faith he had in a dream of one organization so planned as to provide a channel through which Baptist churches may work together in carrying out the will of God.

Swift progress toward this ideal was being made before Rice's death in the various state conventions. As the General Convention moved farther away from the denominational plan, the state bodies, especially in the South, took the opposite direction.

The Convention had not only restricted itself to missions to the heathen, but it also continued in the trend to make the will of a few leaders dominate the policy of the entire body. From the Board of Managers elected at each triennial meeting, an Acting Board was selected with almost complete executive power. These were all residents of the vicinity of Boston, and while their devotion to the mission cause cannot be questioned, they were certainly not representative of the denomination as a whole. They began to speak of themselves as the Baptist Board of Foreign Missions.

It cannot be too strongly stated that these leaders were sincere men who had a genuine love for foreign missions, and who honestly believed they were serving in the best manner. Most of them had never approved of an actual denominational convention and had thought of the General Convention as a foreign mission society, the chief function of which was to raise money with which the Board might carry on a mission program in accordance with their own judgment. Dr. Daniel Sharp, who served as a member of the Board for thirty-two years, expressed this sentiment clearly as the idea he held from the beginning.

Not all of the founders of the Triennial Convention had such a conception of the body. W. B. Johnson, Richard Furman, and others hoped to make the Convention representative of the denomination. Rice's dream appealed to their own conception of a general body based ultimately upon the churches and sponsoring many phases of Christian work. Now Rice and Furman were dead. But in the South were many men who refused to give up the struggle.

Sooner or later, those who advocated a general organization similar to the state conventions in constituency and scope of activity were certain to form such a body. This sentiment was openly voiced in the West and in the South. The abolition movement which began to gather rapidly increasing strength after 1835 provided the occasion for the new organization.

The Acting Board plainly stated in answer to a question proposed by the Alabama Convention, that it would under no circumstances appoint a slave owner as a missionary. Since the Convention had affirmed that slavery was not a matter upon which it would take a position, this answer seemed to many an evidence that the Board felt no obligation to conform to the will of those who had elected them.

A call was immediately sent out requesting a meeting to consider the forming of a new convention. It was addressed to the Baptist churches of Virginia and "the Baptist denomination of the United States generally." The invitation suggested that not only foreign missions, but publication work, theological education, and "several important subjects" might be considered at the meeting. One might almost feel that the spirit of Luther Rice had a hand in planning the call!

In South Carolina a special session of the state convention was called to consider the invitation. W. B. Johnson was president, and in his address he called for consideration of "one convention, embodying the whole denomination together with separate and distinct boards for each object of benevolent enterprise, located at different places all amenable to the Convention."

At the historic meeting held in Augusta, Georgia,

May 8, 1845, it was Johnson who was appointed chairman of the committee to draft the constitution. In 1813 he had written an appeal to the Baptists of Georgia and South Carolina to join in a meeting in "some central situation of the United States for the purpose of organizing an efficient and practical plan on which the energies of the whole Baptist denomination throughout America may be elicited, combined, and directed in one sacred effort . . ." This expression of "a plan for eliciting, combining, and directing the energies of the whole denomination" occurs again in the constitution of the General Convention of 1814, for Johnson was a member of the committee which prepared it. He had not changed his idea of such a general body, and the constitution adopted by the Southern Baptist Convention in 1845 stated that organization was formed "for the purpose of carrying into effect the benevolent intentions of our constituents by organizing a plan for eliciting, combining, and directing the energies of the whole denomination in one sacred effort for the propogation of the Gospel."

The Convention was to "promote foreign and domestic missions and other important objects connected with the Redeemer's Kingdom."

Doubtless the influence of Dr. Johnson, who was elected president of the Southern Baptist Convention, had much to do with this adoption of the denominational rather than the society plan. He had long advocated this program of Christian work.

Dr. W. W. Barnes in *The Southern Baptist Convention,*

1845-1953, gives this evaluation of the new Convention:

> The members of the consultative convention at Augusta returned home after having proposed a new sort of convention, an organization the plan of which was more in accord with the ecclesiology prevalent in the South. It was such an organization as Luther Rice and Richard Furman desired in 1814. . . . . Such an organization as had been functioning in the several state conventions. It was truly a denominational convention comprehending within its scope any phase of work, missions, education, benevolence, etc., that the convention should desire to perform.

As early as 1815 Rice had stated that one of his chief aims was "to open a channel of intercourse between the Board and all the Baptist churches in the United States." The constituency of the Augusta Convention of 1845 would have delighted his heart. Of the 184 Baptist religious bodies represented in the meeting, 166 were churches. Years were to elapse before the Southern Baptist Convention should by constitutional provision be composed solely of messengers from churches. However, from the first meeting, church representatives far outnumbered all others. The Convention was to serve as an agency for "Baptist churches in the United States." Although not expressly stated, it was taken for granted that the general body was to respond to the will of the churches. Article IX even went so far as to speak of the "churches composing this Convention." Since the Convention was designed to serve as an agency through which each church could function in the whole Christian program, and since the work of the Kingdom is not a sectional matter, no thought was entertained of a geographical limitation.

The invitation to join in the new undertaking was extended to all who could accept the principles which called forth the organization. In one of the addresses occurred these words: "Our language to all America and to all Christians, if they will hear us, is 'come over' and for these objects as you love souls 'help us.' " The call or invitation for the consultative meeting stated clearly, "We wish not to have a merely sectional convention . . . We cordially invite all our brethren, North and South, East and West . . . We are desirous to see a full Convention. Let us brethren have a meeting concentrating in a good measure the wisdom, experience, and sentiments of the denomination in the South and Southwest, and such portions of our brethren in our places as may deem it best to unite with us."

The idea of such a Convention was attractive to many who did not live in the South. Distance, the difficulties of communication, and the rapidly increasing sectional tensions prevented the enlistment of churches in the North, but there was no idea to exclude them because of their location.

The foreign mission program, which was launched at once, has always been first in the hearts of Southern Baptists. It is the growth of the Convention itself in numbers and influence that has made possible a continually enlarging endeavor on the foreign field.

There was a clear intention to expand geographically.

In the minutes of the organization meeting it is stated, "One thing is certain; we must go everywhere preaching the Word." It is true there was an emphasis on the territory of the slave holding states, of the South generally. This was natural since one of the complaints against the Home Mission Society was that the South had been neglected in the appointment of missionaries. In the 1850 report the Domestic Board, after stating, "The domestic field extends from the Atlantic to the Pacific, from the Great Lakes to the Gulf of Mexico," added, "In the dispensation of Providence, the southern portion of this field has been made our *immediate* (italics added) sphere of labor."

From the time of the second triennial meeting in 1849 of the Southern Baptist Convention, the messengers called for an expansion of home mission labors far beyond the territorial limits of the traditional South. At this session the Committee on New Fields for Domestic Missions reported, "The only new territories that present themselves are the newly acquired territories of California and New Mexico." Concerning California the reports state, ". . . it is absolutely important that the work should be commenced forthwith."

In 1855 the Southern Baptist Convention authorized its Board of Domestic Missions to take over the work of the American Indian Association, and immediate steps were taken to strengthen the missionary operations in Indian Territory. At this session the Convention passed the following: "Resolved that the Board of Domestic

Missions be instructed to occupy Kansas as a field of missions as soon as practicable."

By this time there was a vigorous work in California. The Convention had shown it was to be limited in its sphere of labor only by the extent of its ability to answer an appeal for help coming from any needy field. Work in the new areas prospered and continued expansion seemed inevitable, but this growth did not come without encountering many difficulties occasioned by indifference and open opposition to the Convention program of home missions.

Many years before, Luther Rice discovered that the carrying out of the Great Commission required an intensive work continually prosecuted in the homeland. He had an overwhelming longing to return to the foreign field, but he soon came to see that he could do much more to make possible the evangelism of the heathen if he gave his life to the building of a great denomination that could continue a mighty program of missions long after he was gone. Rice's greatest contribution was not the sums he raised for the foreign mission cause, nor the men and women whom he won to full surrender as missionaries. By arousing and organizing Baptists for a united effort in founding and nurturing New Testament churches he did a work that has continued to bless the whole wide world.

The old General Convention had refused to follow Rice's leadership and had reverted to the status of a foreign mission society. Then in 1832 a similar agency for promoting home missions was formed called the

American Baptist Home Mission Society. It was, as its name indicates, based on the society rather than the denominational idea of Christian work.

During the very first year of its existence the Southern Baptist Convention was in danger of committing the same error made by the first Triennial Baptist Convention. Although a Board of Domestic Missions was elected and officers designated, the work had a very discouraging start. Before the 1846 meeting a president, two corresponding secretaries, and a treasurer had either resigned or refused to serve. The Board report for 1846 states, "These changes in the acting officers of the Board, almost paralyzed its efforts and at one time threatened its overthrow."

D. P. Bestor gave the following as his reason for resigning: "I have learned by visiting many, and by an extensive correspondence, that our brethren prefer carrying on their domestic missionary operations through their associations and state conventions. They approve invariably of our southern organization, but I cannot persuade them to act efficiently in its support. Someone should be employed who can be more successful than I have been; who can induce the associations and the churches to unite with the Board, and to pour their funds into a common treasury."

It would have been a crippling, perhaps a fatal blow to the Convention had this spirit of opposition to a centralized and uniform program of home missions won the day. In a general denominational body which seeks to forward the entire program of Christian work, there must be some agency which draws the churches together in a uniform or common plan of activity. As needs arise some agency must be available to answer the call for help until the general organization can create a specific agency to meet the need. With no executive committee, no Sunday School Board, no inter-agency council, and no central committee for establishing new work, the Convention would have been well on its way to becoming another foreign mission society.

Russell Holman, a graduate of Brown University, who had shown his zeal and missionary spirit by establishing a Baptist church in strongly Catholic New Orleans, was persuaded to accept the secretaryship in December, 1845. The work immediately began to prosper. By 1860 the Board had 116 missionaries on the field.

The work done by the Domestic Board in the older states was of great importance in promoting the idea of a corporate denominational consciousness as well as in establishing new churches. However, it was in the newer territories that its work stands out more clearly.

Luther Rice had dreamed of the time when the wild West would be filled with cities and farms. He saw the importance of winning the settlers to the cause of Christ, that they in turn might unite their strength and zeal with that of their eastern brethren in the common task. He realized the stable and conservative East could blend with the energetic and progressive West to the mutual advantage of both and for greater efficiency in the Redeemer's work.

The Southern Baptist Convention leaders of those early

days saw this truth. In the 1846 session much was said concerning the need of the work in the new state of Texas. James Huckins and William Tryon were named in the Board's report as its appointees. It was stated that they were raising funds "for the erection of houses of worship in Galveston and Houston, their destined field of labor." Attention was also called to Austin, Matagora, San Antonio, and the part of Texas east of the Rio Grande.

This interest in the Lone Star state continued. For the next several years the Convention minutes recorded the labor of new workers, and the Board pointed with pride to the success of its missionaries. In 1852 Texas churches in Houston, Huntsville, and Montgomery were reported to be self-supporting and Galveston was soon to be.

In *Home and Foreign Journal* for June 1852 is found this item:

Immigration Into Texas
1. From all the southern states, according to the most reliable accounts they are flowing into Texas with unsurpassed and probably unexampled rapidity. Of these a large proportion are Baptists in sentiment, many of them members of our churches.

The article concludes with the warning that what Southern Baptists do in the matter of missions will decide the future of the state!

In the 1853 report on Texas the Board declared "on it (Texas) your Board has for a number of years expended more labor than on any other state." A glowing report of the progress of the work was then given including the forming of a state convention which would be self-sustaining.

By 1860 Texas Baptists had become so strong the Board had only three missionaries serving among them. A state convention was in existence which reported more than 30,000 members of Baptist churches.

The Board's admonition concerning the future had been wisely heeded! The money spent on home missions in Texas was already paying rich dividends in a steady stream which has continued to multiply.

In the Indian Territory the work flourished during these years preceding the War Between the States. H. F. Buckner, the apostle to the Creeks, saw multitudes won and baptized. Willis Burns, A. E. Vandiver, James A. Preston, and R. J. Houge worked faithfully among the red men. In 1857 Joseph Samuel Murrow was sent to the territory as a missionary of the Domestic Board. He witnessed on the Indian mission field in Atoka, Oklahoma, until his death in 1929 — a span of service covering 72 years. After 1891 he was an appointee of the American Baptist Home Mission Society.

The first Southern Baptist home missionaries arrived in California in 1854. During the next six years at least 15 missionaries were appointed by the Domestic Board to serve in that state. Under the leadership of J. Lewis Shuck, who had earlier served as a missionary to China under the Triennial Convention, they organized churches and associations, published a paper, and carried on a general missionary program. The early California churches were very missionary minded and very loyal to the Southern Baptist Convention.

In the Convention minutes for 1855 California is commended for exceeding in gifts to home missions Tennessee, Arkansas, Texas, Kentucky, Louisiana, North Carolina, and Florida. For three years the total gifts to the Southern Baptist Convention causes from California greatly exceeded the corresponding total from Texas, although the number of Baptists in California was much smaller. What might have been the result today had it been possible for the Domestic Board to have continued its aid to California for a few years!

A home missionary of the Southern Baptist Domestic Board moved to Marin County, California, in 1859 and soon erected a building and established a school which he called San Rafael Baptist Institute. J. Lewis Shuck wrote concerning the institution, "Here is a fine beginning for a Baptist Theological School." The Institute soon died but 100 years later the prophecy came true when Golden Gate Baptist Theological Seminary was established in Marin County near the site of Gilbert's school.

In 1860 the prospects seemed bright indeed for the continued expansion of Southern Baptist work. The Home Board (still called the Board of Domestic and Indian Missions) had established itself in the thinking of the denomination, and its work was prospering in the West as well as in the traditional Southern states. Luther Rice's conception of a great denomination working in a united effort to take the full Christian message to all of the world seemed on the verge of complete fulfillment!

V

THE DREAM COMES TRUE!

The darkness flees, the night is past,
The light of day now gleams and glows;
The dream of old comes true at last,
And brighter still the vision glows.

ISAAC TAYLOR TICHENOR, the popular pastor of
the First Baptist Church of Montgomery, Alabama,
was reading the latest issue of the *Home and Foreign
Journal,* dated February 1855. A very pleased expression
came over his face as he noted the following item:

> Missionary to Oakland City, California
> At the December meeting of the Domestic
> Board, Rev. E. J. Willis was appointed their
> missionary to preach in the new city of Oakland
> opposite San Francisco in California. Brother
> Willis is a lawyer by profession, but the Lord
> having called him from the law to the gospel
> and all of the Baptist ministers of that region
> having recommended him, the Board voted his
> appointment unanimously.

When a deacon dropped by to discuss a business matter involving the church, the pastor gleefully called his
attention to the article.

"I am happy to see that the Board at Marion (Alabama)
is sincerely seeking to carry out the will of the Convention
which has been expressed so clearly. For six years we

84

have been calling for a mission program in California," he said.

"But, Brother Tichenor, I thought J. Lewis Shuck was sent out there more than a year ago."

"Yes, but an effort was made to restrict his work to the Chinese. Only in the last few months has the Board really pressed the work among the Americans. Of course, the work with the Chinese is important, but even Shuck sees the tremendous importance of a greatly enlarged work among the people who have thronged into the state from the East."

The pastor's voice grew husky, as it always did when he spoke while under the strain of a deep emotion. A severe attack of the measles when he was 16 years of age had permanently affected his vocal organs.

"California has commercial advantages and an extent of territory far greater than most easterners realize. The rapid increase of its population continues unabated. At the first meeting of the Southern Baptist Convention which I attended, it was reported that thousands were pouring into the state and that within a few years its inhabitants would be numbered by the millions.

"That was in 1849 and the committee on New Fields for Domestic Missions recommended that work be started at once."

I. T. Tichenor had never seen Luther Rice. He was an 11-year-old boy when Rice died; but he shared the conviction of the latter that all phases of the Redeemer's work depend upon strong, functioning New Testament churches. He was even more convinced than Rice that

85

the foreign mission movement could be successful only if the home base was kept strong and continually expanding.

He treasured the memory of that Convention session of 1849. He was only 23 years old at the time and was serving as pastor of the First Baptist Church of Columbus, Mississippi. He and Deacon Mullins made the journey to Charleston, South Carolina, to attend the meeting. For several years he had suffered very poor health, and was so thin he weighed only 120 pounds. He had already made a name for himself in Mississippi, and the good deacon embarrassed his pastor by telling and re-telling the story of how a maiden lady in the Columbus church after a glorious service of unusual power had thrown her arms around Tichenor and shouted, "God hath chosen the weak things of this world to confound the mighty."

His reputation had preceded him to Charleston, and in spite of his youth he was appointed to the important Committee on Agencies. He was also selected to bring the Sunday afternoon sermon, and from that day until his death he was recognized as a leader among Southern Baptists.

Although he served for many years as a pastor, Tichenor was always deeply concerned about the denomination's mission responsibility. His first Christian service was as a representative of the American Indian Mission Association. It was he who served as chairman of the committee which in 1852 called for sending missionaries to California "as soon as possible."

So enthusiastic was he for the development of Baptist work in the West that he resigned his work at Columbus and went to Texas for a series of meetings before accepting the call of the First Baptist Church in Montgomery, Alabama, in December, 1851.

As pastor of this important church he exerted all of his influence for a strong, general, denominational body. Mr. and Mrs. J. H. Priest were serving as missionaries in Africa under appointment of the Foreign Mission Board with their salaries paid by the Alabama Association. Because of some difficulties with the Board the missionaries sought to persuade the Association to support them directly and independently. Tichenor led in opposing such a plan. He was convinced the Redeemer's work could best be advanced by loyal co-operation with the Convention organization, and he never wavered from this conviction.

He rejoiced when the work of the American Indian Association was taken over by the Southern Baptist Convention. As reports continued to reflect Southern Baptist growth in Indian Territory, Texas, and distant California, the future looked bright with promise.

Tichenor was also one with Luther Rice and Richard Furman in their concern for promoting theological education among Baptists. When Southern Baptist Theological Seminary completed its first session in 1860, it was Isaac Tichenor who brought the baccalaureate sermon, using the text, "who is sufficient for these things?"

Rice's vision of one general convention sponsoring all benevolent objects had not actually been attained in the existing organization. The seminary was not established by the Southern Baptist Convention, although many demands had been made for the Convention to take such a step. The educational convention which authorized the founding of the school met in Louisville, Kentucky, two days before the 1857 meeting of the Southern Baptist Convention. From the beginning the seminary was thought of as a Southern Baptist institution, but many years were to elapse before it legally became an agency of the Convention.

The Convention had not entered the field of publication and Sunday school promotion. The Southern Baptist Publication Society of Charleston, South Carolina, was formed in 1847 and provided literature for the churches of the South. The idea of separate societies for different objects was still advocated by many Southern Baptists. However, the feeling of a corporate denominational consciousness was growing stronger and stronger. The Convention went so far as to propose the union of its own Bible Board with the Board of the Southern Baptist Publication Society, just as if they were two boards of the same Convention. Undoubtedly the society method for conducting denominational enterprises was passing away.

Then came the awful catastrophe of war. For four long years the southern states tasted the bitterness of invasion and blockade. The Convention's program of expansion was abruptly halted; yet, in those years of trial two steps were taken that were indications of the path the Convention was to follow. The first was the founding of a Sunday School Board in 1863.

The second was the action of the Board of Domestic Missions in adjusting itself to existing conditions and performing a needed task. No organization can ever fore-see all of the needs which it may be called upon to meet. Baptists have discovered the importance of having some agency which can be used to carry an unexpected bureau until either the need is passed or a new agency is created. The Domestic (Home Mission) Board has played this part throughout history.

The particular task which claimed its attention during the war years was ministry to the soldiers in the armies of the Confederacy. Dr. J. B. Lawrence in his *History of the Home Mission Board* gives a graphic and thrilling account of this work. Some of the greatest preachers among Southern Baptists were among the 137 missionaries employed by the Board in this work.

When the long conflict was ended, the trials and hardships of the South were only begun. For the next ten years the economic situation in the southern states not only prevented any expansion for Southern Baptists but actually caused steady losses.

Dr. M. T. Sumner, secretary of the Domestic Board, worked enthusiastically to re-open mission stations and support the languishing work of home missions. Southern Baptists responded hopefully to the call for mission funds, but as time passed there appeared no improvement in the financial picture in the south. It was inevitable that the Domestic Board should face a decrease in receipts.

Yet the need for its work was greater than at any previous time. In 1873 the Convention voted that Sunday school work should be combined with the work of home missions. The official name of the Board was now the

Domestic and Indian Mission and Sunday School Board. This was shortened the following year to the Home Mission Board.

The Board inherited a debt from the Sunday School Board, and it was instructed by the Convention to continue the publication of Sunday school literature without obligating the Convention or any of its boards. This difficult assignment came at a time when there was an increasing protest against the efforts of the Board to raise money!

The state conventions were hard pressed in attempting to support their own work, and it seemed to some the money collected by agents of the Home Board could be more profitably used in the program within the states. There had been a feeling of resentment against the use of "agencies" from the first year of the Convention's existence. To have the representatives of different boards competing with each other for funds among the churches was much like having separate societies canvassing the same field.

There was no plan for regular systematic support for mission causes, so the use of agents had continued. Now in this time of economic crisis, opposition to this method of fund-raising increased until some state conventions denied Home Board representatives the privilege of soliciting contributions within their territory. Vainly the Home Board sought to work out some plan of co-operation between itself and state conventions or associations. It was unable to supply enough aid to regional bodies to make such co-operative efforts mean much to the local groups. As the fortune of the Home Board ebbed lower and lower the actual existence of the Convention itself came into jeopardy. It seemed the society method of doing benevolent work might yet prevail, even in the South. Two northern societies were vigorously pushing their work in the Southern states.

Even before hostilities had ceased the American Baptist Home Mission Society had begun work among the ex-slaves. During the Reconstruction days this work was increased, and before long other areas of service were entered. Since the impoverished South could not undertake anything like an adequate home mission program, many people, both in the North and the South, began to advocate the expanding of the Society's program southward. In most cases, at least at first, the Society's workers came into the South at the urgent invitation of Baptists already in the area.

A study of the entry of the northern agency's representatives into the Indian Territory reveals this quite graphically. Clearly, the movement was in response to an earnest appeal for help.

The few Southern Baptist missionaries who returned to the Indian Territory after the war found the task too great and the workers too few. The need was more acute than ever before, both among the Indians and among the whites who were coming into the Nations. In 1871 H. F. Buckner wrote, "I have written to the Home Mission Board at Marion in vain. I suppose they are pressed for funds. There is not another Baptist missionary in this Nation."

At the 1875 meeting of the Choctaw and Chickasaw

91

Association, the following preamble and resolutions were moved, and after a full and free discussion unanimously adopted:

> Whereas we have heard from the reports of the Committee on Missions, of the great destitution in the bounds of an Association, which embraces the whole country of the Choctaw and Chickasaw Nations of Indians, and which facts we know to be true . . .

> Resolved, that this Association formally and sincerely invite and request the Home Mission Society in New York to enter into this field and help the few who are now laboring here in our great work by sending missionaries among us and adopting and supporting our native preachers.

The American Baptist Home Mission Society accepted the invitation and became the strength and support of Baptist interest in the Indian Territory. By 1899 it had expended more than $200,000.00 in the eastern half of what is now Oklahoma for missionary, school, and chapel building work. This was in full accord with the voluntary principle so dear to Baptists. When a Baptist body desires affiliation with another Baptist body which is willing to enter into such a relationship, there is nothing improper in such action. The Home Mission Board of the Southern Baptist Convention took no exception to, nor entered any protest against, the action of the Choctaw and Chickasaw Association noted above.

For the first few years there seems to have been no resentment among Southern Baptists toward the idea of the Home Mission Society entering needy fields in the

South. So far as Indian Territory was concerned there was either complete indifference or tacit approval.

A plan of co-operation between the various state conventions and the Home Mission Society was worked out. The American Baptist Publication Society entered with zest into a mighty endeavor to establish its work in the South. Soon the efforts of these two northern societies overshadowed all others in a Sunday school and home mission program in the South. Had this trend continued the Southern Baptist Convention would probably have passed out of existence.

Among those who were greatly disturbed by these possibilities were such men as John A. Broadus, and J. B. Jeter; also I. T. Tichenor, who while pastor at Montgomery, Alabama, had taken such a strong position on the matter of loyalty to the Convention and its boards.

Dr. Tichenor, in 1872, had become president of the State Agricultural and Mechanical College (now Auburn University) located at Auburn, Alabama. He had a steadfast faith in the future economic and industrial greatness of the South. He earnestly desired a comparable spiritual greatness to accompany this material growth. He did not believe the northern societies could lead Southern Baptists in such a development in nearly so effective manner as could their own Convention. However, if the society method was to supplant the Convention the change must be faced! If the Baptists of the South did not see the necessity for preserving their own organization and methods then the next best thing was to see if they were ready to take full advantage of all the help that could be received from the societies.

As President Tichenor gravely considered these matters, he decided to force the issue. The Southern Baptist Convention was to meet in 1879 at Atlanta, Georgia. He determined to attend the session and introduce a resolution that would be decisive. The 1868 session had voted, ". . . That the Southern Baptist Convention is a permanent institution," but this had not averted the decline. Tichenor decided to introduce the idea of a fuller cooperation with the societies in words that might imply an eventual organic union. He seems to have taken no one into his confidence before making this startling proposal.

In a sense the issue facing the Convention was the same one which confronted the old Triennial Convention in 1826. In addition to the immediate problems was the principle championed by Luther Rice, Richard Furman, and W. B. Johnson — the denominational rather than the society method of doing denominational work. But these stalwarts who had stood for the convention method were no longer present, and many of the messengers saw only the surface and secondary issues which confronted them.

The situation seemed weighted decidedly in favor of the Societies. From 1865 until 1880 was, as has been noted, the darkest period in the Convention's history; but the North had greatly prospered during these years while the South was recovering from the Civil War. While the powerless and impoverished Home Mission Board had been unable to answer calls for help, the American Baptist Home Mission Society had responded with a generosity that caused its popularity to rise rapidly even in the heart of the South.

94

The resentment against the North was greatly softened when the Mission Society and the Publication Society employed southern men as their agents and missionaries. While Tichenor clearly saw that this movement would eventually destroy the Convention, many who did not agree with him were weakening the Home Mission Board and hastening the ruin of the Convention which they loved by affiliation with the American Baptist Home Mission Society.

On the opening day of the Convention Tichenor presented a preamble and two resolutions calling for the "dead past to bury its dead" and for a joint meeting between representatives of the Baptist bodies of the United States to promote "the more efficient working of the Baptist brotherhood."

It was referred to a committee with Tichenor as chairman and brought up for discussion on Saturday morning, May 10, 1879. So intense was the feeling in the Convention that twenty-three speeches were made concerning the resolution. Tichenor's address in support of his motion exhibited all his powers of eloquence, for he was determined to give every reason which the advocates of such a measure could offer.

Shortly before adjournment in the afternoon, a motion by Dr. John A. Broadus to strike the two resolutions was carried. This decision carried the promise that the plan of the general session to promote the work of the denomination would continue.

Important as this action was, it would have been useless unless some means had been devised to strengthen the

Home Board. That this was recognized is shown by the Home Mission Board report accepted by the same 1879 session. It affirmed the absolute necessity for the Board's existence. After calling attention to the work of preaching in destitute places and of aiding state conventions and associations in their work the report gave as another of its functions:

> To give unity to our work, and to harmonize all state organizations with our plans and modes of operation, so as to prevent collision between State and General Secretaries, it is important that there should be a common organ for communication, co-operation, and general aims for the attainment of our great mission. The Home Mission Board of this Convention will probably have work to do until the millenium dawns in the world.

By 1882 the conviction that the actual continued existence of the Convention depended upon a successful home mission program had so possessed Southern Baptists that the Convention appointed a committee to consider carefully the condition of the Home Mission Board and bring recommendations to improve its usefulness and enlarge its work. The committee recommended among other things that the office of the Board be removed from Marion, Alabama, to Atlanta, Georgia. This was adopted by a vote of 222 to 13. The same year the offices opened in Atlanta, I. T. Tichenor was elected corresponding secretary of the Board.

For eighteen years he led in a program of continued enlargement. His faith that the life of the Southern Baptist Convention is bound up with the work of the Home

Mission Board was amply justified. He won the state conventions from alignment with the northern societies and promoted a spirit of loyalty to the complete work of the Convention. He worked hard to develop a more satisfactory plan of co-operation with the state bodies, and soon the Southern Baptist Convention began to exhibit a spirit of unity and progress that seemed almost miraculous.

Tichenor believed God had committed the religious destiny of the world to the English speaking people. Since the majority of them lived in America, it was his contention that winning this land to Christ was of major importance. He was fond of saying, "We challenge the Christian world to the proposition that the evangelization of this country is among human affairs, the mightiest factor in the world's redemption."

Even more than Luther Rice he believed it was imperative that Baptists prosper in America that other lands might hear the gospel through their ministry.

Under his direction the Home Board offered its services to perform any needed service for which no other agency was responsible. Sometimes a venture of this type proved so successful that it came to require more attention than the Home Board could give it, and a new agency had to be created. When the time came he was always willing to have the Home Board surrender the work that it might be advanced in some better way. He had led in developing a series of Sunday school helps that were a source of income to the Board. However, when the time was ripe he threw all of his influence behind the movement to establish the present Sunday School Board in 1893 to which he gladly turned over the work.

When a door for mission work was opened in Cuba and the Foreign Board was unable to enter he led the Home Board to sponsor a very successful missionary work in that island. Since his time the Board has continued this policy of helping where help is needed and then surrendering the work when its assistance is no longer required. In teaching, in evangelism, in church building, in missionary work in new territories, in city missions, and in mission work among the mountain people his aims have influenced those who have followed him. When he retired in 1899 the work of the Convention was so firmly established that its marvelous growth has continued.

Perhaps the most obvious thing connected with Southern Baptist growth since his time is the territorial expansion far beyond the limits of the old South. For many years this was largely an expansion westward as Baptists from the South moved toward the Pacific in quest of new homes, land, or jobs. More recently there has been a great movement to the cities of the North. The industrial plants, the oil fields, the mines, and the lumber camps have attracted millions from their southern homes. Hundreds of thousands of these were members of Baptist churches and have sought to perpetuate in their new homes the type of church organization, forms of worship, and denominational affiliation with which they are familiar.

In the early years of the Southern Baptist Convention life, there was little tendency to identify a particular sense of uniqueness with the general denominational body. Baptists were distinct from other denominations; but those Baptists who were working through other missionary bodies were considered as sharing in this uniqueness. Most people thought of the Convention simply as an agency through which the churches might do their mission work. But as has been shown, there was from the beginning a provision made for a centralized effort for doing all phases of the Kingdom work through one organization — the Convention. Through the establishment of new boards and commissions this plan of work has thrived among Southern Baptists.

The more fully a general denominational body fosters the complete program carried on by the local church, the greater becomes that area in which the churches conform to the same pattern. If churches work together only in foreign missions they may differ greatly in many ways. If they follow identical programs in missions, education, Sunday school work, training, promotion, women's work, laymen's activities — all sponsored by one general convention, they will tend to become more and more alike. The literature, the visits of denominational workers, the general meetings, and the study courses will continue the trend so that common terms and methods become part of the definite pattern of church life. In growing more alike these churches, of course, grow to differ more and more from those which do not follow the uniform pattern. Soon the standard program is so accented that members with such convention affiliation feel lost and on unfamiliar ground in a church without such affiliation—even though both groups accept the same confession of faith. Of course, if there is even a suspicion of a slight doctrinal difference, its importance is greatly magnified.

It may be logically argued that a Baptist familiar with such a set pattern should forget it when he moves to a locality where churches follow some other form of alignment. But the familiar terms have become precious — a part of "the language of Zion." They are associated with the forms of worship and service. If he should attempt to fit into a church of a different pattern he may actually create more problems and tensions than if he finds a few others like himself and begins a new church which will work within the framework familiar to him.

For years an effort was made to devise some plan of comity that would restrict Baptists of any one locality to affiliation with a particular denominational body. Experience has demonstrated that it is unwise to attempt to force alignment on a Baptist group. Just as there are no rigid "parish boundaries" among Baptists, there are no associational or convention boundaries. The place where one lives does not determine his religious affiliation.

During the last fifty years as the work of the Southern Baptist Convention has expanded to the West and the North, the denominational plan which Rice advocated has continued to prosper. The Home Mission Board has increased its ministry to the cities, the language groups, the frontier region, and in general to any area where there is a call for service and a willingness on the part of the Convention to answer the call.

A plan of co-operation with the various state conventions has been devised which is working with gratifying success.

A deepening appreciation for the ministry of the Home Mission Board is being shown. Never was it more important to use every means available for evangelizing America and filling it with churches founded on the New Testament pattern and composed of members trained to do the work of Christ. Since people from all nations of the earth are found living in the United States an opportunity for world missions is found at our very door. Dr. Tichenor's statement "that the evangelization of this country is among human affairs, the mightiest factor in the world's redemption" seems even more evident in our day.

Rice's desire for denominational sponsorship of ministers' education has come true. The Southern Baptist Convention now has six theological seminaries. Their operational expenses are provided by the Convention. College and university training has been left to the state conventions.

The northern societies began the movement toward a closer corporate denominational union soon after 1900. In 1907 the Northern Baptist Convention was formed. In spite of many difficulties this organization has moved continually toward a more centralized form of denominational work. Luther Rice's plan seems on its way to realization in this great body, which in 1951 changed its name to the American Baptist Convention.

As the year 1964 approaches, the Baptists of America are looking back with gratitude and appreciation on 150 years of organized mission work. The great Jubilee Advance program was launched in 1959 to climax the one-hundred and fiftieth anniversary of the founding of the General Missionary Convention of the Baptist Denomination in the United States of America for Foreign Missions. It is impossible to give any serious thought to this epoch-making event without realizing the key position Luther Rice occupied in uniting the Baptists of this land in obeying the command of our Lord.

How he must rejoice today to know that his vision lives on in the hearts of millions of Baptists. In every section of our land and in seven great general denominational bodies of North America his work is bearing fruit today —not only in America, but throughout the earth.

His dream lives on!

Questions

CHAPTER I

1. What opposition did Luther Rice face?
2. Why was it necessary for Rice to travel from association to association to secure support for missions?
3. What was the dream and vision which Rice had for Baptists in America?
4. Who were some of the other Baptists who dreamed of missions, and what were their dreams?
5. What was the purpose of the early associations since they were not organized to foster missions?

CHAPTER II

1. Where was Rice born? Describe his early childhood.
2. Of which church was Rice a member?
3. Where was Rice educated, and what was his connection with the "Society of Inquiry on the Subject of Missions?"
4. Why was not Rice appointed a missionary at the time Adoniram Judson and the others were? How did he secure appointment?
5. What happened on the way and after arrival in India that changed the life of Judson and Rice? What was Rice's reception when he returned to America by the Baptists?

CHAPTER III

1. What other causes did Rice want the General Missionary Convention to foster?
2. Who was John Mason Peck and what was his connection with Rice?

3. What was Rice's connection with Christian education?
4. What was the big disappointment to Rice which occurred in the life of the Convention?
5. What was the *Latter Day Luminary* and Rice's connection with it?

CHAPTER IV

1. Did Rice discontinue his labors in raising money for missions when dismissed by the Convention?
2. Where and when did Rice die?
3. In what way does the Southern Baptist Convention embody the dream of Rice?
4. What were the first fields of endeavor for the Southern Baptist Convention?
5. When and what type work was first started by Southern Baptists in California?

CHAPTER V

1. How did the Civil War affect the Board of Domestic Missions of Southern Baptist Convention?
2. Who was I. T. Tichenor, and what was the question he raised at the 1879 Southern Baptist Convention in Atlanta, Georgia?
3. What were some of the results of Tichenor's leadership of the Home Mission Board?
4. What effect has a denominational program had upon church members moving to other sections of the country?
5. What is the Baptist Jubilee Advance, and what connection does this have with the General Missionary Convention?